Connecting in Philadelphia

*512 Great Places to Enjoy Yourself
and Meet New People*

by

Ruth B. Harvey, Ph.D.

Published by
OFFTIME PRESS
P.O. Box 29158
Philadelphia, PA 19127-9998

Connecting in Philadelphia

If you are unable to find this book in your bookstore,
you may order directly from the publisher:
OFFTIME PRESS
P.O. Box 29158
Philadelphia, PA   19127-9998

Layout and Design: Judith A. Brandy
Cover Design and Illustration: Marta Williamson and Nick
                                    Tridemas of Tridemas Studios
Editors: Kathy Sheehan, Sharyn Flanagan, and Eleanor Burtis

ACKNOWLEDGMENTS

A few people worked very hard to get this book in print. These people did an inordinate amount of work in a compressed period of time and each made significant contributions to the production of this book.

Starting at the beginning, Grace Culbertson worked with me to get the massive mess of data entered into an organized file. It was amazing how similar our thinking was about the numerous decisions that had to be made at that tedious stage. We also mastered the Macintosh together. Her gentle encouragement kept the book going.

Writing a book is hard. Self-publishing it is murder! Great people to help you sure make a difference. During countless hours of work, Judith Allyson Brandy taught me everything I never wanted to know (but had to) about publishing a book. Besides offering invaluable insight and evaluation about it's content, she designed and executed the layout, added artistic *pizzazz* and guided in all phases of production. Without her, this would still be a list in my Macintosh. She has also become a very enjoyable friend!

The editors worked over a manuscript that was given to them in pieces, and returned it in record time. Each of them taught me something useful about how to write. Sheehan (Kathy) reduced sentences like a madwoman, took out a thousand parentheses (and exclamation marks) and inserted sarcastic remarks in the margins!!!! She took time out from her faraway paradise and got back in touch with her old friend around this project. Sharyn Flanagan was fast and efficient with eyes like a hawk. She offered many encouraging comments as well as excellent editorial changes. Third, I have been blessed to have the finest grammarian in Philadelphia as a member of my family, my aunt, Eleanor Burtis. Hopefully, there is a number of more times you will be red penciling my writing in the future, Eleanor — it's like you were my personal editor! We have awesome conversations, besides! (Put the red pencil away, Eleanor — it's done!) Any remaining mistakes are all mine.

The contributions of artists Nick Tridemas and Marta Williamson cannot be underestimated. When they showed me Marta's illustrations and the classy front cover, I realized this was going to be a **real** book. The energy and life conveyed is exactly the feeling I hope comes through in the text.

Although they were not actively involved, I want to thank my Dad (Bob Ballentine) for teaching me the value of being excited about the Keystone Trails Club. My Mom (Helen Ballentine) has an irrepressible energy when it comes to talking to and enjoying people. She taught me a lot about having fun and expecting the best. My kids, Rachel and Dave have supported my endeavors through thick and thin, and been proud of the results. More than that, they have shown me a lot about following my passions and including quality fun time in my life. Thanks, too, to Jim's kids and their wives, Gene & Carol, and Ted & Tammy, for knowing how important this has been to me and being so supportive. I also want to thank my teacher, Faye Soffen, who has continuously urged me to go for the Golden Opportunities in my professional life.

Most of all, I want to thank Jim, who listened to every detail and nuance, thought about and gave wise counsel on the problems, and sympathized when I needed comfort. He has been unwavering in his view that this book was well worth the effort and could be a valued resource. He was confident and reassuring and gave love all along the way. It is the greatest affirmation to the ideas in this book that I found such a terrific partner by my connections in Philadelphia.

Contents

Biking in Fairmount Park with Philadelphia Art Museum Class. Photo by Kelly and Massa.

FINDING THE PEOPLE YOU WANT TO MEET BY CHOOSING THE ACTIVITIES YOU LOVE

INTRODUCTION: THE SHORT VERSION

Here is an outline of the philosophy of this book for those of you who want to speed read to the key points.

1 - There are some GREAT places to enjoy and meet people in Philadelphia,
2 - There are some neat people to meet there,
3 - You have a much greater chance of meeting "your" neat people if you join them to do your favorite activities,
4 - You can identify those with the personality traits you seek with greater accuracy if you go to a group that has a focus and meets regularly,
5 - To maximize happiness, you need to engage in interest-activities you truly love, join the community that does them, and have a lot of fun!

The introduction that follows elaborates these ideas and provides a **mini-workshop** on how to develop a great social life. You're on your own now!

INTRODUCTION: THE REAL ONE

This book is for people who want to get off the couch and out of the house to join others who are enjoying life's healthy pleasures. This includes single people, people who are new to the area, people who want to have more compatible people (friends and lovers) in their lives, and people who love socializing but need new ideas for things to do and places to go.

♦ The Workshops, the Participants and the Importance of Choosing the Right Places to go

The activities listed in this guide have been selected because they facilitate interaction between participants. They were found in public sources: Fliers, brochures and notices from local papers and magazines which listed various places to do things with other people. The collection was organized and passed on to people in my workshops about discovering places to meet people of interest, both friends and romantic partners. The participants suggested that a full list be printed in book form — so this is it!

Attending the workshops were people **new to the area**, both single and attached, who already had identified interests. They wanted to know where to find people their age and people who participated in their favorite activities. They wanted to know what great things were going on in the city and where interesting people gathered. Some people wanted to know where to do weaving or play bridge, others wanted to find groups who go cross country skiing or biking in Valley Green. They wanted good current information about these things as well as the best resources for keeping up with what's happening in Philadelphia. That was easy!

Other people just wanted to **expand their repertoire** of exciting things to do, things to try, and possible new interests to include in their lives. They might have needed a nudge to *try* acting in a play, joining a poetry writing group, or giving Cajun dancing a whirl. Even with their busy lives, they were ready to grow and do something new. Many were eager to explore new interests. Some just wanted the "where's" and "when's." Others sought names of groups they hadn't heard of.

Identifying specific places to go was especially important to the **singles** participants who believed the answer to finding romantic relationships was in knowing WHERE to go to find the right people with whom they could have a rich and satisfying life. In all honesty, I had to agree. Finding the right place(s) to go helps a lot. It's pretty hard to find the people you want to meet in a laundromat, even if you have great people-meeting skills! (How do you start *that* conversation: "Excuse me, but I think you're using too much clorox...")

No, it's clear to me that the best chance of finding people who have durability as friends and loving partners is in places where you have common interests. For starters, you know that they independently chose an activity that you really enjoy. If the relationship continues, you already share an important bond. You also know more about someone's personality when you have been involved in a mutual activity for a while because you have a chance to see how they act in different situations. Your interest in them will be based on more than just looks! And, speaking of interest, don't you think you are your most interesting and attractive self when you are enthusiastically involved in something you love to do? Isn't that "the you" that you would like people to want to connect with? One last point: When two people are doing a purposeful activity, people-meeting skills pretty much take care of themselves. You just feel more natural approaching someone when you have an activity-based reason to talk to him, rather than having to start with a free floating "opener."

The people in my workshops taught me a lot. They taught me people want to grow even when it can be risky. They taught me that it's never too late to look into a new interest or develop a new hobby. They taught me that people really like to be with other people, no matter how much they complain about each other's annoying habits. They taught me about the significance of our "leisure lives" and how much they matter to being happy and mentally healthy. Indeed, I learned from them that the success of our social lives often determines whether we judge our lives as happy or not.

◆ Happiness and Choosing Interests

What they were telling me fit in with the ideas I was reading in a book called **Flow**. People are happiest when they are immersed in doing something they love, according to this book. So happy, that they are oblivious to time and their surroundings.

The significance of this point for me is that it affirms the powerful influence of people's activities on their feelings, attitudes, and general disposition. <u>What</u> people are doing and the rewards and risks of that activity, <u>who</u> they're with and the kinds of interaction they're having, influence how they feel about themselves and life in general. This means you can influence moods like boredom, frustration, self-depreciation, hopefulness, excitement, vitality by paying attention to your schedule of activities!

It's interesting how little attention many of us pay to developing interests and activities we could enjoy. In the workshops, I use an interest list to help jog participants' memories of activities they have liked at some time in their lives. I have included here a brief version of that list.

If you already know the kinds of things you love to do, you don't need this list. You are ready to go forward. If, however, you know you'd like to do some exploring but have not identified the direction, then this list probably will be useful.

LEISURE ACTIVITIES SHEET

Acting
Archery
Backpacking
Baseball
Bicycling
Billiards
Bird watching
Camping
Canoeing
Swimming
Carpentry
Car Repair
Ceramics
Checkers/Chess
Civic Organizations
Collecting: Stamps
    Coins, Antiques
Cooking
Dancing
Electronics
Films
Fishing

Folk Dancing
Football
Gardening
Games: Outdoor
Golf
Hiking/Walking
Home Repair
Jigsaw Puzzles
Jogging

Judo/Karate
Kite Flying
Motor Boating
Motorcycling
Music
Painting/Drawing
Playing Card Games
Political Activities
Play & Poetry Read
    Organizations
Religious Organizations
Roller Skating/Blading

Sailing
Sculpture
Sewing
Singing
Singles Groups
Skiing
Squash/Handball
Surfing

Table Tennis
Taking Pictures
Tennis
Theater
Tours/Galleries
Volleyball
Watching TV
Weight Lifting
Window Shopping
Woodworking
Yoga

Exercise: You could circle interests that engender a spark. Once you've identified the activities that look interesting, you can look in the listing to get some leads about where they might be happening. Call and have a friendly chat with the contact person to get a picture of what the group actually does, who goes there, what kind of commitment you have to make, and other questions that matter to you. Most groups are very proud to discuss their activities, and are interested in and welcoming toward prospective new participants. You can also ask them about other groups involved in similar interests.

♦ Balancing your Activity Choices

Using many parts of yourself. The first type of balance relates to our personal make-up: We have personalities very rich and multifaceted, with many sides to each one of us.

> We have a *serious thoughtful* side that reflects and contemplates important questions.
> An *adventurous side* where we are exhilarated by the challenge of hiking a mountain or sailing a storm.
> A *comic, silly, playful side* that loves to goof off and for all the world feels like 10 years old.
> An *intellectual side* that loves to analyze and play with ideas and possibilities.
> A *flirtatious, sexy side* that loves courtship games.
> A *soft romantic side* that loves candles and illusion.
> A *curious, tenacious part* that won't let go of a problem until it is resolved.
> And on and on.

I think that lethargy and boredom, sometimes even depression, are related to times when we get in a rut, when we use some part of our personality to the exclusion of others. It is also depressing when we spend most of our time doing things that don't really interest us but are what other people think we should be doing. We feel sluggish when we only seem to have time for what we *have* to do, and no time to do what we *want* to do.

That's when we feel narrowed down. We may feel bored

with the world and our friends but we may be also bored with ourselves. If we slide into filling our time with the same-old, same-old things then we stop expanding. We stop looking at new places in the world, and stop **using new parts of ourselves** with the new people we meet there.

I think it's very important to be aware of that slide. I think it's important to be actively involved in trying to expand your knowledge of places to go and things to do that give you vitality and enthusiasm, that give you that "can't wait to go" feeling. You want to have a variety of experiences that arouse curiosity, adventure, and a deep and sincere interest.

Exercise: First of all you can choose activities that appeal to different sides of yourself. I divided some of my interests into three basic personality parts.

PHYSICAL	INTELLECTUAL	CULTURAL
hiking	SCRABBLE	public art
dancing	book discussions	First Friday
sailing	world affairs discussions	sketch club
biking	Alliance Francaise	singing

Put the activities you chose on the Leisure Activities Sheet into categories that reflect these parts of you. It was hard for me not to get out of balance in favor of physical activities. I could see that I might spend all my time involved in these types of events and undervalue the parts of me that love good discussions and singing. When this happens, I restrict the types of people I am meeting and lose touch with those valuable parts of myself, parts I really enjoy. When I feel out of balance and notice a feeling of "missing something," I know it's time to look at the way I'm spending my leisure-life time.

Ongoing activities or one-time events

Another type of balance has to do with the way the activities are organized. Some activities are one-shot events, such as singing in the Sunday afternoon **Sing-In** with **Singing City,** while others are ongoing with a regular core of people, like the **Temple Center City Chorus**.

This is a pretty important distinction. Single people complain they "go out a lot but don't meet 'anybody,'" thus drawing the conclusion that there is no one 'out there' to meet. If you ask where they are going, you find out they are going to various one-time events over and over. When they <u>do</u> talk to people, their conversations are often brief and the subject matter is often of little importance to either person. How do they know WHO they've met? Ongoing activities give you a chance to get to know someone and develop a relationship based on something more than first impressions.

Activities with structured interaction vs ambiguous format

One-time events are fun too, especially if they have a focus. Which brings us to the next important characteristic of these activities: how **structured** are they? Some are very organized around the activity. You are there to do something and that is what you do. If you attend a Cajun dance class, you will team up with a partner, receive instruction, and dance together! In this case, even though it might be only one class, you have a chance to see if you enjoy the dancing without making a major commitment, and you can participate in engaging interaction with some of the people there.

Activities that are more loosely structured (e.g., **First Friday**, or **River Blues** at Penn's Landing) are tougher places to meet people. However, there are many times when your time is tight, and flexibility and spontaneity are your first priorities in deciding how to spend your day. Fortunately, these activities provide a focus that you are sharing with other people there. However, the lack of structured interaction means you have to take a lot of initiative to meet someone. Although one-time events which are loosely structured are the hardest places to find compatible people, that is what most of us generally do. Then we wonder why we have to sort through so many people to find a few that interest us!

Risky and exciting or familiar and comfortable

Another dimension to keep in balance when choosing an activity is your psychological safety-excitement continuum. This is something that changes from day to day. Some days you feel that you can handle anything (or anyone), and other days you feel that you just want to be in the bosom of familiar friends. What's important is that you take a reading of your "risk tolerance" and choose accordingly. You need to watch that you include activities all across this scale—things that expand your boundaries and are therefore more risky sometimes, and things that are familiar and nurturing other times. If you only go places that feel completely safe (from rejection, for example) your social life can feel flat. Activities that include a stimulating challenge and adventure such as an exploratory hike or trying a new sport are important to keep the roses in your cheeks.

By the way, when I talk about risk and safety, I am talking about psychological safety. At no time should you engage in activities where there are serious compromises to your physical safety. That isn't exciting; that's stupid.

◆ ◆ ◆

◆ Your Social Goals

Suppose you have identified your interests and have been going to a lot of places to do them — but you're not finding the people who interest you. They could be people you like, but they are not the community (or person) you are looking for.

The next step in this process is to define your social goals. Whom do you really want to meet? This is a tricky question, but one that has to be addressed directly in order to choose the places that will satisfy you.

First of all, how do we **describe the people we're looking for** in a way that helps us find them? Often we describe them by detailing the personal traits we want them to have. But how do we *find* them? It certainly would be nice if we knew the places where the sweet people were, where the sensitive people were, the kind, considerate and good looking people were, and best yet, where those who had ALL of these qualities hung out! Unfortunately I do not know those places! However, I do think that interest-based activities attract people with certain types of personality characteristics, don't you? So looking at where they spend their discretionary time may provide one of the best clues we have to finding people we like. For examples: if someone physically fit appeals to you, try outdoors activities; if you want someone who loves ideas, try world affairs groups or book clubs; someone who cares about political change, look in political organizations; people who are nurturing, look in care-taking volunteering, and so on.

Secondly, be **clear with yourself about what you are looking for** (friends, romantic partners, biking buddies). Analyze where those people might be, and make a commitment to keep looking until you find them. If you are wishing to go with a group that shares your social conscience, look into community service activities and try them. If you are looking for a wife, think about where women appropriate for you to marry might be. Check groups for singles with a special interest sub-group, and then go with the idea of having fun while you look. If you want to find people to discuss books with, make a commitment to explore the various book discussion groups until you find the one you want. I am interested in finding women friends who enjoy outdoor activities, especially golf, but if I find a great women's hiking group, that's OK too. The clearer you are, the more specific your search can be and the more likely it is that you'll find your people.

Third of all, watch out for **perfectionism**. You certainly are entitled to be as much of a perfectionist as you wish, but the higher your standards, the fewer people will make it through your filters. You'll need to weigh the importance of finding friends or partners to do things with against your expectations for the people you find. A really good book for singles on this subject is by Judith Sills, ***How to Stop Looking for Somebody Perfect and Find Someone to Love.*** Myself, I have always had lots of imperfect friends, just right for imperfect me. It means I have had a chance to try lots of things with different people and groups, without expecting all the qualities I like to be in one person or place.

The beauty of identifying who you want to meet is when you can put it together with your own interests. For example, I now play golf with my husband and his friends which I truly enjoy. But I also want to meet local women golfers as well. Besides, I am interested in finding more women to hang around with who enjoy outdoors activities. So I found the **Executive Women's Golf League** and **Womanship**, women who sail together.

There are many interest groups that are specifically for certain populations. They might be for certain ages, religious denominations, races and genders. When you know who you want to meet, you can make more of an effort to go places you love where you think they might be.

♦ Suggestions to Help You Get Going (or, dealing with your resistance)

1. Do whatever you need to do to **Commit** to finding great places for yourself, for finding both activities and ongoing community. To find what you're looking for, you have to invest energy and time and maintain the optimism that you will find what you want. You will have to evaluate each situation. When one place you try doesn't work out, try another, and hang in there knowing that you're getting closer to the places you really want to belong to.

2. **Collect Information and Make a List.** Call and write for catalogs, fliers and brochures. People love to send them. Scan the local papers (*Welcomat, City Paper*, Friday's *Inquirer* and *Daily News*, your local paper) frequently. Every week is best. After 10 years of looking, I'm still finding new things every week. Write down the activities and groups that appeal to you even if you are not quite ready to go. Look at them often. Try the easiest, then one a little harder, and so on. Keep a notebook about the ones you liked. Talk to people and ask them where they go to have fun and meet people they like.

3. **Confront your Myths—demons and expectations—**about the people who are socializing in the places you'd like to go. Hold them to the cold light of day and see them realistically. Look at these black and white examples: "Everybody who goes to Singles groups is bottom of the barrel, desperate or secretly married;" or, "The love of my life is waiting for me at this event. If she's not there tonight, I'm never going again." These attitudes may sound pretty silly on paper, but negative attitudes that keep you in your living room often sound this way and operate underground. It is only after you become aware of them, and talk to yourself about them, that you will

defuse them. That gives you the freedom to go out and enjoy the people you meet.

4. **Plan.**   Choose places that look good, but feel safe enough. Make sure you go with someone you can trust, but who will give you space if you want it. Discuss it before you go. You might want to drive your own car so you have the assurance that you won't be 'stuck' in a situation. Find an outfit you feel really good in (women and men!) and have it ready ahead of time. Know your familiar excuses to cop out and plan a self-talk response to them.

◆ ◆ ◆

◆ Socializing HOT TIPS

Try to **be open to people who don't fit your favorite visual stereotype** at first. You would be surprised at the qualities people have underneath the image. The most successful approach in socializing is an attitude of LIKING PEOPLE. Sound corny? Well, watch people in social situations. Who would YOU want to talk to? What does this attitude look like? You can't even begin to *like* someone without *looking* at them, *listening* to them, and enjoying them for what they are. You will be projecting interest and energy and a general good humor about the situation!

Try to **get *into* the activity!** This is important! You are here to have as much fun as you can. To be immersed, to get into "**FLOW**," act as if this was the thing you always wanted to do! You give yourself a chance to get out of observing yourself ("Look how stupid I look.") and into the game! It is the only way to find out if this is something you could really love.

Not only that. Research shows that you are most attractive and interesting when you are engaged and interested in what's going on, in something outside of yourself. You are more approachable and people feel more comfortable with you — which is what they want to feel.

Pay attention to cues when you want to approach someone. What did they say or do in the group that interested you? Comment on it or ask about it. You can also look for identifying information such as jewelry or logos on T-shirts that tell you what this person cares about, and remark on it.

Use the group activity to get in connection with people there. Offer to join someone in a project, or ask for help in learning something the group is doing. When I go to a Swing Dance I always ask an expert to dance one dance with me so I can get the feel of how it's supposed to feel. I've never been turned down, even though they may have regretted it while dancing! If you *want* to be involved, most people will extend to help you in a gracious manner. Remember that chatting with someone is not a commitment!

Learn to deal with rejection. You are going to get slighted, rejected, and disappointed. Sometimes, you'll feel fearful that you do not belong. Most of the time it's just part of the game—everybody gets rejected and the more you are in contact with people, the more it happens. You need to work on how not to take it personally. Learn about this by talking to friends, reading about it, and taking workshops like mine where it is addressed. We all need armor and strategies to stop fears about rejection from keeping us home.

Keep in mind that many people feel anxious and awkward. There is a common human concern called the "on stage" phenomenon in which you are sure that everybody is looking at you with a very critical eye. Usually the criticism you think they have is the one you have about yourself. The fact is that someone *may* be looking, but his main concern is usually how *he* is appearing to the crowd. Knowing that others are uneasy about the impression they make on *me* makes it easier for me to relax.

Sometimes the "on stage" feelings are labeled shyness, as in, "I'm too shy to try that." Can we talk for a minute about shyness? Most people are shy sometimes, especially in unfamiliar situations when they don't know anyone. The feeling is based on not knowing what in the world to do or say and to whom. One of the reasons for this book is to encourage people who are moderately reserved to go places where the situation liberates their natural friendliness. Many times shyness is more related to the situation than the person! Test this out by being aware of your fluttering anxiety when you go places of different risk value to you. Do you notice your "shyness" level change?

Finally, give yourself **permission to leave** at any time when you have given an event a fair shot and you know you aren't having a good time. It's much easier to *go* if you know you don't have to spend hours and hours feeling miserable if what sounded great turns out to be lousy. There are lots of great places for you out there, and many that do not work at all. That's OK—go sort them out!

◆ ◆ ◆

◆ Final Note

My father is even smarter than I thought. He told me that if people are lonely they should join the Appalachian Trail Club. I was single at the time and thought that was the dumbest thing I ever heard. I didn't want to go hiking. What I wanted was to meet a handsome man and get married. Over the course of a very interesting 16 years of singleness, I was lucky to have a wealth of terrific experiences doing new activities that others led me to. I began energetically exploring the city to find the things *I* loved. There were many! And *doing* them were many wonderful people. Now, as a married person, I'm still doing them!

The process of finding new interests, new places to have fun and new people to join with *is* exciting. Like any challenge, it takes thought, energy and nerve. You'll learn a lot about yourself—and I mean things you do not know now! It is about your own self-development, regardless of whether you have an intimate partner, children or close friends. One of the best things about it is that the skills you learn while exploring this great city will *always* be with you, no matter what happens to you or where you are. This is a golden opportunity!

Ruth on the Appalachian Trail offering proof that she got the message.

How to use this book

1. This guide contains an overview of participatory activities in a number of interest categories. It does not include every group and activity in Philadelphia. (There are many, many more!) It is meant to provide you with kick-off material to get you thinking and started on your unique search!

2. Places close down. They change structure and focus. Contact people change. Please call before you set out. I worked very hard to have phone numbers current to time of publication. (However, I found errors even to the very end, after many edits. So, be kind.)

    It was very hard to accept the discontinuation of several groups, like Temple Cinemathetique. One or two are still included in this guide with a "No Longer" note next to the name. I just could not let them go. My fantasy is that if enough people call in support of the event, it will start up again. People power.

3. Every place in the guide is not in Philadelphia. (I cheated.) The entire VACATIONS & ADVENTURES chapter lists places away from Philadelphia. Also, there are some 10 other "get-away" places listed, usually camps specializing in a participatory activity. Please don't be offended. I chose places where many Philadelphia-area people go — people not necessarily next door, but whom you may otherwise wish to meet!

4. Note that there are sometimes two phone numbers and two addresses. When that is the case, the first address-phone number is that of the organization, and the second is that of the place where the activity is held. You should CALL the organization to find out more about the group and details of the events, but you should GO to the location address.

5. Have a great time!

ART

Classes
Classes, Films & Discussions
Gallery Programs
Organizations
Tours
Workshops

ART

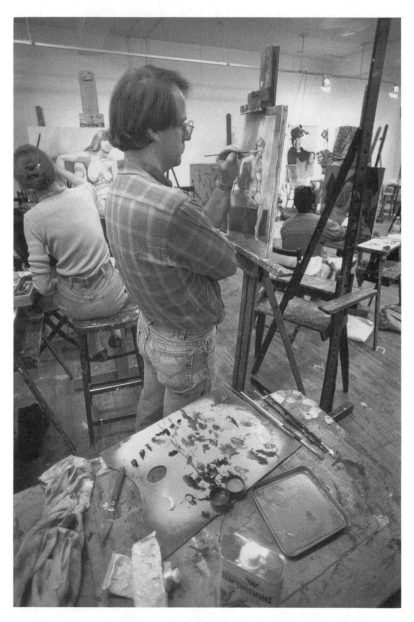

Painting class at the Samuel Fleisher Art Memorial. Photo by Mark Garvin.

When I think about "doing ART" with other people, I think about two types of activities: *MAKING ART* and *LOOKING AT ART*.

In *MAKING ART*, maybe the biggest thing we all have to deal with is that we don't have to be "good at it." In that way it's like SINGING and DANCING — we've been taught that if you aren't really "good at it" ("good" being what your art teacher pronounced after you did a picture), then you have no business doing it. Many of us never allowed ourselves to play around with soft drawing pencils, water colors, or those nifty pastel chalky crayons you see in the expensive art stores. The message has been, "Live your life without doing art because you don't do it 'right'..."

WAIT A MINUTE!

If you <u>like it, do it</u>! Do it just because *MAKING ART* is fun and fulfilling — and because the product is a unique expression of yourself, which is reason enough to do it. Do it and find the artist in you. Do it for whatever reason you want to.

Besides, while you are having fun getting involved in ART, you will find others who are enjoying it also. You'll find people who also are embarrassed that they don't do it "good" enough, people who love color for the sheer beauty of it, people who also strive to brush a soft peachy shadow on the apple. You'll all want to talk about what is happening with your artwork in the class, and, painting side by side, you'll form a community around that activity.

The best news is that there are wonderful classes in the area for learning how to do all kinds of ART. A notable example in South Philadelphia is the **Fleisher Art Center** where for a low cost you can take classes in Painting, Sculpture, Photography, and others. Local suburban art centers, such as

Cheltenham and **Whitemarsh,** have all kinds of art classes, such as Jewelry Making and Weaving, as well as the traditional classes in Painting and Drawing. The **Mt. Airy Learning Tree** has a class in String Figures for adults <u>and</u> kids. Remember Cat's Cradle and Jacob's Ladder? Sam Dorfman will patiently teach you those and many more for the huge fee of $11 for three sessions! And if you don't think you meet some neat people in <u>that</u> class...! This listing is just the tip of the iceberg of informal classes in the larger Philadelphia area.

The city's universities (such as **Moore, University of the Arts, Temple** and **Penn,** non-credit) and art schools (such as **The Arts League**) offer unusual and traditional classes, such as Children's Illustrations, Printmaking, Paper Making, Interior Design, Pastel Washes, and the like. The **Art Institute** offers Workshops for "Art in the 90's" and **International House's Folklife Center** has workshops in Folk Crafts. For Ceramics, a great place is the **Clay Studio** which teaches novices like you and me, and advanced potters as well. So if you don't already "do ART," choose your medium and jump in!

When you get serious about something, you often wish you had a group or organization through which you could develop your interest and ability. Such organizations exist both for the newly initiated and masters of their craft. For example, the Clay Studio is the home of the **Philadelphia Ceramic Consortium**, a group that supports all phases of the artistic growth of its members. Similar groups include the **Plastic Club** (they do Drawing and Painting, not plastic!), and the **Print Club**.

LOOKING AT ART, which is wonderful as a solitary experience, is an exciting way to connect with another person. Just looking together and knowing about the beauty you both see can be a great thing to share with someone. Not only that, you

can also have some terrific discussions about the historical context, the lines, the artistic unity and general questions ("What IS it?"). As with MAKING ART, the knowledge or skills you possess are not the issue. Loving ART is not an IQ quiz. Anybody can love what they see. Artists do art for everybody, not just other artists or Ph.D.'s in Art History. (Of course, like anything else, the more you know, the more dimensions you may enjoy, but we all can appreciate ART at *any* knowledge level.) And one bonus of being open to enjoying ART is that there are lots of others who are interested too, whose company you may well enjoy, if only when you feel like going out to LOOK AT ART.

In Philadelphia, there are scads of terrific galleries, shows, programs and organizations that promote wonderful ART. Two programs that strike me as outstanding for meeting others interested in LOOKING AT ART are:

First Friday, which takes place on the first Friday of every month in Olde City North. A large number of galleries (usually about 70) open their doors that evening for viewing and receptions for the general public. You make your way from gallery to gallery along with many others whose priorities include setting aside a Friday night for ART observation. Great conversations and friendships have been known to develop out of an evening of such potential. However, even if that doesn't happen for you, what has happened is a chance to see some of Philadelphia's really fine artworks.

The **Art Lovers' Exchange**, in which there are many single people, is a group that explores local art exhibits together. They hold classes, workshops, lectures, and visits to area-wide galleries. An organization such as this one provides activities that encourage conversation and networking with other people who love art.

There are many excellent programs to attend and organizations to join in the area. For example, consider the lunch time discussions at the **Academy of Fine Arts**: for a dollar donation (even includes coffee!) you can hear some fine presentations from contemporary artists. Other programs include the **Philadelphia Art Alliance** which sponsors regular showings with supporting discussions and lectures, the **Print Shop**, and the **Friends of the Goldie Paley Gallery** to name a few. Another group, **Excursions from the Square** which leaves from Rittenhouse Square, tours art events in the outlying areas, including gardens, art openings, and fancy mansions.

You must be wondering why no mention of the most famous of our art institutions — the **Philadelphia Museum of Art.** I mention it last because it has everything mentioned above: classes (*about* art, not *doing* it), films, lectures, an organization to join for the support of its fine programs, and special events galore. The most well-known event is on Wednesday night: "Art Around the World," which revolves around a theme and includes hanging art, films, lecture-discussions and food. If you call the museum, you can obtain a brochure which lists the themes of each Wednesday night event in advance.

The activities listed in this chapter are ongoing in some fashion. But there are scores of one night events open to the public, listed regularly in the *City Paper* and the *Welcomat.*

Check Them Out!!

CLASSES

❏ Abington Art Center

515 Meetinghouse Road
Jenkintown, PA
(215) 887-4882

Comments: A large number of classes and art activities are offered here. Classes include: Drawing, Painting, Photography and others.

❏ Barnes Foundation

300 Latches Lane
Merion, PA
(610) 667-0290

Comments: This is an art jewel of Philadelphia with a fabulous collection including the French Impressionists. They also offer tours, Art History classes, a Landscaping Program, and more.
Date: Friday, Saturday, & Sunday

❏ Cheltenham Center For The Arts

439 Ashbourne Road
Cheltenham, PA 19012
(215) 379-4660

Comments: A fine suburban adult education center with classes in Painting and Drawing, Printmaking, Jewelry, Stained Glass and more.

❏ Clay Studio

139 N. 2nd Street
Philadelphia, PA
(215) 925-3453

Comments: Premier pottery and sculpture studio offering workshops, lectures, exhibits, and classes such as General Pottery (Beginning, Intermediate and Advanced), Handbuilding, Ceramic Jewelry in Colored Clay, and Figure Sculpture.
Cost: About $125

ART

Classes

❑ Fleisher Art Memorial

709-721 Catharine Street
Philadelphia, PA 19147
(215) 922-3456

Comments: Mr. Samuel Fleisher established this school so you could
learn art! Many art classes including Painting, Drawing, Ceramics and
Photography are held during the week, and in May/June there is a
Landscape Painting Class on Saturdays.
Cost: Very inexpensive or free

❑ Main Line Center For The Arts

Old Buck Road & Lancaster Avenue
Haverford, PA
(215) 525-0272

Comments: This <u>large</u> adult education program includes a variety of
visual arts classes. An extensive catalog describes their exciting classes.

❑ Manayunk Art Center

419 Green Lane (Rear)
Philadelphia, PA
(215) 482-3363

Comments: A variety of visual art classes and workshops are offered
in this neighborhood program, such as: Pastels, Printmaking, Introduction To Art Basics, and Model Groups.

❑ Moore College Of Art

20th & Race Streets
Philadelphia, PA
(215) 568-4515

Comments: This excellent teaching institution offers unique art
classes to non-matriculating students, such as: Basic Jewelry Making,
Children's Book Illustrations, Introduction To Interior Design, Calligra-
phy, Wood Carving, and Desk Top Publishing.

❏ Mt. Airy Learning Tree

6700 Germantown Avenue
Philadelphia, PA 19119
(215) 849-5500

Activity Location: *Various locations around Mt. Airy*

Comments: Many, many unusual high quality classes for next to nothing, including: String Figures, Outdoor Pastel Drawing, Teddy Bear Workshop, Origami, Clay Whistles, and Card Making.
Cost: Very reasonable

❏ Philadelphia Department Of Recreation Cultural & Special Events

(215) 685-0152

Activity Location: *Various city recreation centers*

Comments: The City sponsors a number of Ceramics, Painting, and Drawing classes for adults at local recreation centers.
Cost: Free
Contact: Mr. Edgar Brown

❏ Philadelphia Sketch Club

235 S. Camac Street
Philadelphia, PA
(215) 545-9298

Comments: This small club for serious sketchers has been offering fine classes for years. Their classes are on some evenings and Saturday mornings, and often use live models. You need to submit work for review to join this group, but you don't have to be a great artist to be admitted, and you don't have to be a member to take classes there.
Date: 4 days/week
Cost: Very reasonable

ART

Classes

❏ Tyler School Of Art

Beach & Penrose Avenues
Philadelphia, PA
(215) 782-2700

Comments: This well-known school, part of Temple University, offers classes in Computer Graphics, Sculpture, Glass, Fibers, and Ceramics. Weekend workshops also available.

❏ University City Arts League

4226 Spruce Street
Philadelphia, PA
(215) 382-7811

Comments: This West Philadelphia center in a large brownstone building presents a wide variety of classes in the arts, music, and dance. Art classes by a very friendly staff include Sculpture, Clay Heads, Oil Painting, Watercolors, and Figure Drawing.

❏ University Of The Arts

Broad & Pine Streets
Philadelphia, PA
(215) 875-3350

Comments: The Continuing Studies Program has classes for non-degree students in Sculpture, Clay Heads, Oil Painting, Watercolors, Figure Drawing and more. Lectures and slide shows are often given with gallery openings.
Contact: Sarah Swan, Continuing Studies Department

❏ Whitemarsh Community Art Center

Box 76
Spring Mill & Cedar Grove Roads
Lafayette Hill, PA 19444
(215) 825-0917

Comments: Excellent programs in Ceramics, Drawing, Printmaking, Basket Weaving, and more.

ART

Classes, Films & Discussions • Gallery Programs

—— CLASSES, FILMS & DISCUSSIONS

❏ Pennsylvania Academy Of Fine Arts

Broad & Cherry Streets
Philadelphia, PA
(215) 972-7600

Comments: Many terrific events including lectures/discussions ("Quilting"), art history lectures ("Overview Of African American Art"), films ("Daughters Of The Dust"), gallery talks, visiting artist lectures (Will Barnet), and more! Call for fliers.
Cost: Free or cheap

❏ Philadelphia Museum Of Art

26th Street & Benjamin Franklin Parkway
Philadelphia, PA
(215) 684-7580

Comments: The Museum offers ongoing classes/lectures/tours, such as the "Saturday Morning Lecture Series." You can also become a Museum member to be privy to special events. Watch for the latest "Art Around The World" with special programs and films on Wednesday nights.
Contact: Education Division

—————— GALLERY PROGRAMS

❏ First Friday

Area Of 3rd & Arch Streets Galleries
Philadelphia, PA

Comments: Tens of galleries are open for visitors with refreshments and lively activity. A new Philadelphia tradition — this is a great Friday night for art and socializing!
Date: First Friday evening of the month

❑ Philadelphia Art Alliance

251 S. 18th Street
Philadelphia, PA 19103
(215) 545-4302

Comments: Besides their elegant galleries, PAA has outstanding play readings, lectures and music programs. A recent addition is the Dean & DeLuca Cafe for after-program coffee.

❑ The Philadelphia Print Shop

8441 Germantown Avenue
Philadelphia, PA
(215) 242-4750

Comments: This fine gallery exhibits original prints and offers seminars and lectures.
Date: Monday to Saturday   **Time**: 10am-5pm

ORGANIZATIONS

❑ Art Lovers Exchange

P.O. Box 265
Bensalem, PA 19020
(800) 342-5250

Comments: A singles group where you can meet others who enjoy cultural events, especially the visual arts. The group meets in galleries for viewing, presentations, and discussions.
Cost: $42/year for membership
Contact: Ann Keesee

❏ Artist Resource Room Of Nexus

Nexus Foundation For Today's Art
137 N. 2nd Street
Philadelphia, PA
(215) 629-1103

Comments: This vital gallery/organization sponsors many lecture-discussions on art for artists ("Matting Your Art Work"), as well as topics on the state of arts in America ("Recent Political Changes and the National Endowment for the Arts") for everyone.

❏ The Clay Studio

Philadelphia Ceramic Consortium
139 N. 2nd Street
Philadelphia, PA 19106
(215) 925-3453

Comments: If you get on their mailing list, you will be amazed at the high level of activity that happens through this group. Ceramic exhibits, classes and workshops are always going on here!

❏ Goldie Paley Gallery & Levy Gallery For The Arts

Moore College Of Art
20th Street & Benjamin Franklin Parkway
Philadelphia, PA 19103
(215) 568-4515

Comments: The Paley Gallery has exhibitions, lectures, symposia, workshops and performances. Become a "Friend" of the Gallery to support these programs and gain entrance to many special events and gatherings.

❏ The Plastic Club

247 S. Camac Street
Philadelphia, PA 19107
(215) 545-9324

Comments: This 96-year old club welcomes artists working in all media. Classes each morning with a teaching monitor and monthly art shows when you may show your work! Lunch and socialize on Wednesdays.

Date: Monday, Wednesday, Thursday   **Time**: Mornings & Lunch

❏ The Print Club

1614 Latimer Street
Philadelphia, PA 19103
(215) 735-6090

Comments: A cultural organization that presents exhibitions of emerging artists and also offers tours, lectures and demonstrations for the public. You can join and support their group or just attend their programs for the public. Newsletter.

TOURS

❏ Autumn Art Tour

Excursions From The Square
(215) 732-8487

Activity Location: *Leaves From Rittenhouse Square Or The Philadelphian*
Philadelphia, PA

Comments: If you are interested in tours to places of art interest such as the Richmond Museum and Monticello, the Falling Water Museum in Pittsburgh, and art and architecture in New Orleans then this lively group is for you! You can find their upcoming trips listed in the *Welcomat*, or call for their newsletter.

WORKSHOPS

❑ Art Workshops For The 90's

Art Institute of Philadelphia
1622 Chestnut Street
Philadelphia, PA 19103
1-800-Ask-Aiph

Comments: Hands-on evening workshops for beginners, hobbyists and working professionals, all at reasonable cost. Classes include Basic Photography, Airbrush Techniques and Introduction to Video.

❑ International House

FolkLife Center of International House
3701 Chestnut Street
Philadelphia, PA 19104
(215) 387-5125 Ext. 2219

Comments: Variety of craft classes and workshops are given by the FolkLife Center periodically. Watch for them in the *In-House Newspaper* sent out by International House.

ART

— NOTES —

Cheap or Free

Happenings

Robert Montgomery Scott leads a bike tour of the Fairmount Park mansions for the Art Museum. Photo by Kelly and Massa.

CHEAP OR FREE

Most things listed in this guide are reasonable to downright cheap, but this chapter highlights a variety of activities that are "great deals," to let you know that you don't need money to do the things you love. If you want to continue to update your file of events that are CHEAP OR FREE, a fine resource is the *Philadelphia Inquirer's* "Free Events" in the Friday *Weekend* section. As you continue looking through that section for the types of activities that interest you, you will find many inexpensive events. Under "Tours," for example, are listed the **Foundation of Architecture's** tours of different Philadelphia neighborhoods, where architecture and social history are explored, observed and discussed under the tutelage of a knowledgeable, professional guide. They're terrific!

Skimming through this chapter you can see that there are outdoor activities, like bird walks at the **Audubon** and **Tinicum Wildlife Centers**, and cultural events like the **Philadelphia Orchestra at the Mann** — but then maybe you already knew about these! However, did you know about the free concerts at the **Curtis Institute of Music** on Friday nights, or that the **Pennsylvania Academy of Fine Arts** is free on Tuesdays and also has outstanding lunch time presentations and discussions for $1? And did you know that you can take excellent classes for free: such as courses in the natural sciences at **Wagner**, contemporary political/social/economic issues at the **George School**, and gardening at a local Philadelphia branch of **Penn State**?

Some CHEAP OR FREE events are only twice a year — like the Spring/Fall group bike hikes sponsored by the **Philadelphia Art Museum** with Robert Montgomery Scott and other guides who will give you the history of the mansions and gardens in Fairmount Park. Some events are once a month, like regular folk sings held in members' homes with the **Philadelphia Folk Song Society** for a very reasonable membership fee.

CHEAP OR FREE

Going places with themes automatically gives you something to talk to your group fellows about or provides opportunities to collaborate in the event. So playing SCRABBLE, going to a games party, a bird walk: they all give you automatic focus — a reason for comfortable interaction. Even in a more unstructured situation, it is fitting and respectable for a music lover to chat with someone new at intermission about the symphony at the **Mann**, react out loud to a book or photograph in the **Book Trader** (Don't you love the picture of the nude gals in a row?), express yourself to anyone and no one about the boat race at a summer regatta, yell for the home team at a **Phillies game**, or laugh out loud about the greatest toy at one of the fun game stores on **South Street**. The more chutzpah you have, the more opportunity you will find to meet people in places that are CHEAP OR FREE — and the more likely it is that people might look at you funny, too...! Can you risk it?

CHEAP OR FREE

❑ Semi-Annual Bike Tour Of Fairmount Park

Philadelphia Art Museum-West Entrance
Benjamin Franklin Parkway
Philadelphia, PA
(215) 684-7926

Comments: Art Museum President Robert Montgomery Scott and other expert guides lead this bike tour (10 miles). In 1993 they saw the Japanese Teahouse, Horticulture Center, Azalea Garden and several Fairmount Park mansions. What a way to learn about the Park!
Date: 2 Sundays/year   **Time**: 2-4:30pm
Cost: $2

❑ The Henry George School

413 S. 10th Street
Philadelphia, PA
(215) 922-4278

Comments: Classes and sophisticated discussions in economics and social philosophy offered free or very cheap. Examples are Fundamental Economics, Protection And International Trade, The Philadelphia Dilemma, Money And Banking, and others. Real quality for next to nothing. Call for brochure of classes.
Cost: $25/class; Saturday classes are free!

❑ Schuylkill Regatta

BoatHouse Row on Kelly Drive
Philadelphia, PA
(215) 232-2293

Comments: Thousands of rowers from across the country come to Kelly Drive for these boat races. They're exciting! The Drive is blocked off, lots of fans, bikes, frisbees, dogs, runners, all to watch the skulls! In the Spring colleges compete on Saturdays and high schools on Sundays, and in the summer watch for local clubs.
Date: Saturdays & Sundays   **Time**: All day
Cost: Free

❑ Folk Dances & Playparties

Philadelphia Folk Song Society
7113 Emlen Street
Philadelphia, PA 19119
(215) 247-1300

Comments: Besides sponsoring the famous Philadelphia FolkFest every August, PFSS has great folk dances and playparties, folk sings, weekend festivals, all very, very cheap. If you want to go to the FolkFest <u>free</u>, you can be a volunteer! Look under Chapter 10 (Music) and Chapter 4 (Dancing) for more information and call PFSS for fliers.

❑ Getting Down & Dirty: Urban Gardening

Penn State Winter Workshops
Provident Mutual Insurance Building
46th & Market Streets
Philadelphia, PA
(215) 560-4167

Comments: One example of many free programs given by Penn State. They also sponsor Environmental Celebrations connecting gardeners with concerns about earth conservation. Call for newsletter listing all classes and events.

❑ Lower Merion-Narberth Watershed Association

(610) 668-4078

Activity Location: *St. Christopher's Church, Righter's Mill Road, Gladwyne, PA*

Comments: Guided hikes in some of the loveliest areas in the Philadelphia area such as the Bridlewild Trail in Gladwyne. Call for directions.

Date: Saturday   **Time**: 10am-Noon
Cost: Free

❏ Pennsylvania Academy Of Fine Arts

Broad & Cherry Streets
Philadelphia, PA 19102
(215) 972-7600

Comments: An art gallery and school that presents terrific lectures, concerts and films at very low cost, such as bag lunch discussions on art topics. See further description of the Academy in Chapter 1 (Art) and Chapter 6 (Discussion Groups). Call for fliers of upcoming events.

❏ Wagner Free Institute Of Science

17th & Montgomery Avenue
Philadelphia, PA
(215) 763-6529

Activity Location: *Various institutions such as libraries, Franklin Institute & Academy of Natural Science.*

Comments: Free 12-week classes on natural science for the public, including: Anthropology ("Colliding Cultures"), Biology/Medical, Geology/Paleontology ("Dinosaurs and the Age of Reptiles!"), Population Biology, and more. What a deal!
Date: Fall & Spring
Cost: Free

❏ Curtis Institute Of Music

1726 Locust Street
Philadelphia, PA 19103
(215) 893-5252

Comments: Presents wonderful Friday night free student orchestra performances. "Friends" of Curtis attend "Conversations At Curtis" lecture/discussions.

❑ The Philadelphia Orchestra

Mann Music Center
52nd and Parkside Avenue
Philadelphia, PA
(215) 878-7707

Comments: Probably one of the most terrific musical adventures happening in the city — great music under the stars! — and it's free if you send in the coupon from the *Philadelphia Inquirer.* Friendly atmosphere — easy chatting with people on the next blanket!
Date: Summer

❑ Manayunk Market

4120 Main Street
Philadelphia, PA 19127
(215) 483-0100

Comments: Marvelous eating deck <u>outside</u> overlooking the Manayunk Canal and neat fun food shops <u>inside</u>. Very easy chatting place and you are likely to see someone you know. Also, the towpath along the Canal is very interesting and fun to walk or bike along. All is near the Manayunk shops. A great place to "hang out" on a beautiful weekend day.

❑ Audubon Wildlife Sanctuary

Mill Grove & Audubon & Pawlings Roads
Audubon, PA
(215) 666-5593

Comments: Classes in nature subjects, for example, "Turning Maple Sap to Syrup." Also, wonderful group walks with or without lectures. Excellent naturalist community.
Cost: Free

❑ Tinicum National Environmental Center

86th & Lindbergh Boulevard
Philadelphia, PA
(215) 365-3118

Comments: Volunteers lead walks through the marshes and wildlife preserve on the weekends.
Date: Weekends
Cost: Free

CHEAP OR FREE

— NOTES —

COMMUNITY SERVICE

Children and Youth
Civic
Companioning
Consumer Issues
Cultural Organizations
Environmental Concerns
Food Co-Op
Holiday Volunteering
Home Building
Homeless Programs
Medical Volunteering
Media
Mentoring Kids
Neighborhood Organizations
Political Activities
Teaching/Tutoring
Volunteering
Walks/Runs For
Charitable Organizations
Wilderness Activities &
Environmental Action
Zoo

COMMUNITY SERVICE

Wissahickon Trail Club clearing a bike trail in Valley Green in Fairmount Park.

Volunteers with Habitat for Humanity mix mortar for home repair and construction.

PASSING IT ON

What is it about giving our resources and time that lifts our spirits? You always hear people saying that they think *they* got more from "helping out" than the people who received the help. Maybe it's just because being fully engaged with others takes your mind off yourself. Maybe it's because this is a *special kind* of being engaged: When we are voluntarily lending what we have to uplift those who could use a hand right now, it might occur to us at some level that we all have times of strength and times of need — that the human condition is about the ebb and flow of trouble and triumph, and we all take our turns along that wavy line. It *feels* right to reach out when you're in a position of strength and share your current resources. It also gives perspective to have real contact with the world that extends beyond your personal needs and have a working connection with some living, breathing part of your community.

Another bonus beyond the opportunities to expand yourself is that the other people involved in COMMUNITY SERVICE are *also* people who understand those things, people who make time in *their* busy lives (like yours) to care about others and not just talk about it. They don't just look good — they *are* good. When you find people who are busy putting their hands where their mouths are, so to speak, you can see what they really care about, which tells you a lot about them and the values they hold. They can see yours, too.

It's amazing to discover the diversity of activities that you can give your time to! You can mentor (emotionally support, teach, guide) a child (**Philadelphia Futures**), protect the **Chesapeake Bay**, help feed the homeless (**Philadelphia Committee for the Homeless**), build houses for young, eager families (**Habitat for Humanity**), or work for Philadelphia celebrations (events like the "**Welcome America**" celebration when the new Convention Center opened in July '93.) You can work with a national political group (**Amnesty International**), work for a terrific candidate for Congress, or work in your neighborhood with a community organization (e.g., **Lighthouse** in Kensington, or **North Light** in Manayunk). There are many cultural institutions that depend on volunteer efforts, like the **Balch Institute** or the **Art Museum of Philadelphia**. And there are many, many opportunities to provide nurturance, strength and hope to people who are sick or disabled, in hospitals or at home.

I've heard people say they are afraid to volunteer their time because they have so little of it and are worried that they will get pressed into more service than they can manage. I think that the opposite is true: One of the best things about volunteering is the control you <u>do</u> have over what and how you give your time. Most organizations understand the heavy time demands you have and appreciate what time you can give, but it's important to be as clear as possible about <u>your</u> situation so they can develop clear expectations. You should be free to commit a lot of time or very little without guilt, which, of course, means you can wade in slowly or jump in head first and really do a job.

Another concern some have is that they ought to have special skills to be able to help — which is true sometimes and not true other times. If you call and explain your skills, the group can determine if there is a way you could be useful, and you can decide if you wish to participate.

And, as always, a third concern is that you will not know anybody there. Believe me, when there is an important job to do — a wall to spackle and paint, a child to be loved into reading — people get to know each other through the job and feel like buddies in no time.

COMMUNITY SERVICE

By the way, if you want to read about the value of volunteer service — both to the individual and to the community — read Robert Coles' <u>A Call to Service</u>. He distinguishes between different kinds of service and looks at the different kinds of satisfactions from each type. This is an excellent and beautiful discussion.

COMMUNITY SERVICE
Children and Youth • Civic • Companioning

—————————— CHILDREN AND YOUTH

❑ Success By 6

> *United Way Of SE Pennsylvania Volunteer Centers*
> *(215) 665-2474*

Comments: This program promotes healthy child development by enhancing the ability of parents and community to fill the needs of children. Volunteering jobs include: museum guide, raising funds, child assistant, and more! There are numerous volunteer opportunities coordinated by United Way and Women's Way. Ask about them.

———————————————————— CIVIC

❑ Volunteer Hotline

> *(215) 636-1672*

Comments: Volunteers are always needed for Philadelphia festivals, such as the "Welcome America!," the "Freedom Festival," and openings of prominent city structures such as the new Convention Center. Call to find out what events are forthcoming that you can be a part of.

———————————— COMPANIONING

❑ Artreach

> *3721 Midvale Avenue*
> *Philadelphia, PA*
> *(215) 951-0316*

Comments: Artreach trains volunteers to coordinate and assist in helping agency staffpersons take handicapped, disadvantaged, and elderly-in-need to the performing arts. Volunteers receive two free tickets to the performance.
Contact: Joyce Burd

COMMUNITY SERVICE

Consumer Issues • Cultural Organizations

CONSUMER ISSUES

❑ Consumers Education and Protective Association (CEPA)

6048 Ogontz Avenue
Philadelphia, PA (Northeast)
(215) 424-1441

Activity Location: *Jardel Rec. Center, Cottman & Penway Avenues*

Comments: Volunteer to investigate consumer issues, such as utility rate increases. You may be involved in educating others about the issues, or taking part in public hearings. Call before going to Tuesday meetings.

Date: Tuesdays   **Time**: 7pm
Cost: $15/Year to join

CULTURAL ORGANIZATIONS

❑ Atwater Kent Museum

15 S. 7th Street
Philadelphia, PA
(215) 922-3031

Comments: This history museum of Philadelphia has exhibits, displays and terrific workshops, lectures and tours. Also, volunteers are needed to work with visiting school groups, with the Victorian Sampler, or doing office work.

Date: Tuesdays-Saturdays   **Time**: 9:30am-4:45pm
Contact: Pat Silverman to volunteer

❑ Curtis Institute Of Music

1726 Locust Street
Philadelphia, PA 19103
(215) 893-5252

Comments: As a volunteer for this fine musical organization you could adopt a student, be a post-recital reception host, conduct tours of the Curtis buildings, or help in the office and with membership.

❏ Philadelphia Orchestra

1420 Locust Street, Suite 320
Philadelphia, PA 19102
(215) 893-1956

Comments: Volunteering for the Orchestra has you involved in fundraising, education, and special projects such as the Radio-athon, Academy of Music tours and Gala Concert Nite. Many benefits including receptions and events for volunteers.

ENVIRONMENTAL CONCERNS

❏ American Littoral Society

Sandy Hook
Highlands, NJ 07732
(908) 291-0055

Comments: This organization promotes the conservation and study of coastal areas. It is an active group, often taking beach walks, canoe trips, observations of the hawks on the Delaware and field trips to monitor water quality and land use. There is also a Lambertville, NJ branch, part of the "RiverKeeper" network (609-397-3077).

❏ Chesapeake Bay Foundation

214 State Street
Harrisburg, PA 17101
(717) 234-5550

Comments: The Chesapeake Bay is closer than you think and it needs your help. Activities of this protection group for the Bay include field trips (canoeing), a Stream Restoration Program, issue discussions and a newsletter for members that lists events.

COMMUNITY SERVICE

❏ Pennypack Environmental Center

Verree Road at Pennypack Creek
Philadelphia, PA 19115
(215) 671-0440

Comments: "Friends of Pennypack Park" organize clean-up and work projects, and other park activities. They hold meetings about current environmental issues, present speakers and programs. Call Fairmount Park (685-0045, Kate Lapszynski) for a complete list of all the "Friends of...." groups, such as Andorra in Northwest Philadelphia.
Date: 3rd Thursday/month

FOOD CO-OP

❏ Weavers Way Cooperative Association

559 Carpenter Lane
Philadelphia, PA 19119
(215) 843-2350

Comments: A congenial, healthy food co-op where you work together to keep fresh food in the store. This is a community which sponsors fun and interesting events, meetings, and maintains a great networking bulletin board.

HOLIDAY VOLUNTEERING

❏ Holiday Volunteer Network

United Way of Southeastern PA
(215) 665-2474

Comments: Don't be alone during the holidays! Call this hotline to put you in touch with a directory of many volunteer opportunities such as gift wrapping, gathering gifts, making homebound visits, etc.

COMMUNITY SERVICE

HOME BUILDING

❑ Habitat For Humanity

1829 N. 19th Street
Philadelphia, PA 19121
(215) 765-6070

Comments: A nationally famous group organizes and instructs housebuilding crews who turn buildings into homes for people with low incomes. You can be experienced or a novice and be <u>very</u> useful here. Nice group of people, too.
Contact: Margo

HOMELESS PROGRAMS

❑ Philadelphia Committee For The Homeless

802 N. Broad Street
Philadelphia, PA 19130
(215) 232-2300

Comments: Major organization in Philadelphia that performs many activities including food distribution and assisting homeless persons in important ways.
Contact: Andrea Ohaviano

MEDIA

❑ Kids Corner and Other Shows

WXPN
(215) 898-6677

Comments: Volunteers with good communication skills answer phones and represent WXPN at concerts and events. Get to know the DJ's and other volunteers.

MEDICAL VOLUNTEERING

❑ AIDS Task Force

1642 Pine Street
Philadelphia, PA
(215) 545-8686

Comments: There is a way we can help fight this damn disease. If you go to the above locaton you can discuss with a counselor the kinds of ways you can be helpful.
Date: Weekdays   **Time**: 9am-5pm

❑ Graduate Hospital Volunteer Service

One Graduate Plaza
Philadelphia, PA 19146
(215) 893-2278

Comments: A variety of volunteer opportunities are available in areas like dietary service, information desk, and social work. You might visit patient rooms with a library cart or work on special projects like the Rittenhouse Square Fair. All hospitals welcome volunteers — try them.

❑ Cuddlers Program

Thomas Jefferson University Hospital
11th & Walnut Street
Philadelphia, PA
(215) 955-6222

Comments: You can cuddle, feed, or read to babies here! Jefferson offers a variety of other volunteer positions as well.

❑ Wissahickon Hospice

8835 Germantown Avenue
Philadelphia, PA 19118
(215) 247-0277

Comments: A cadre of trained volunteers provides a full range of important services to dying patients and their caregivers.
Contact: Rosemary McCade

COMMUNITY SERVICE
Mentoring Kids • Neighborhood Organizations

MENTORING KIDS

❑ Philadelphia Futures

230 S. Broad Street
Philadelphia, PA 19102
(215) 790-1666

Comments: You can help a kid stay in school, do well and prepare for college. Futures offers training and meetings with other mentors.

NEIGHBORHOOD ORGANIZATIONS

❑ Community Outreach Partnership

C/O Trinity Memorial Church
2212 Spruce Street
Philadelphia, PA 19103
(215) 732-2515

Comments: This group provides shelter, food and resources to local area residents.

❑ North Light Community Center

175 Green Lane
Philadelphia, PA (Manayunk)
(215) 483-4800

Comments: One of many neighborhood centers which sponsors projects and classes useful to the neighborhood. Many socializing opportunities and mixers while you're getting things done.

COMMUNITY SERVICE

❑ Olde City Civic Association

Betsy Ross House Building
239 Arch Street
Philadelphia, PA 19106
(215) 440-7000

Comments: One of many neighborhood organizations which enjoys support from community members. They hold meetings to discuss local issues about community development and historic preservation. They also have a social committee and neighborhood parties six times a year.

❑ Old Pine Community Center

401 Lombard Street
Philadelphia, PA 19147
(215) 627-2493

Comments: This community center has activities for area residents, including a variety of classes (crafts, games, etc.) as well as socializing opportunities. Get to know your neighbors!

POLITICAL ACTIVITIES

❑ Amnesty International

(215) 387-9331

Comments: Group discusses issues and takes action on political projects. They hold letter-writing meetings and speaker-discussion events.
Date: Monthly

❑ Democratic Party

(215) 241-7800

Comments: You can join the political party of your choice and actively help your candidates be elected. Or you can choose a candidate and independently work for her/him.

COMMUNITY SERVICE

❑ Young Republicans

(215) 333-3282

Comments: You can join the political party of your choice (or a subgroup like this one) and actively help your favorite candidates be elected.

TEACHING/TUTORING

❑ Center For Literacy

IBM Building
1 Commerce Square, 2005 Market Street
Philadelphia, PA
(215) 474-1CFL

Comments: This group will train you to tutor adults and children in reading and then will help connect you to a teaching situation.

❑ Mayor's Commission On Literacy

1500 Walnut Street (18th Floor)
Philadelphia, PA
(215) 875-6602

Comments: A City program that organizes volunteers to teach reading to those who want to learn.

VOLUNTEERING

❑ United Way of SE Penna Volunteer Centers

(215) 665-2474

Comments: If you're not sure what kind of volunteering you want to do, this major umbrella organization refers you to agencies that need the kind of service you are interested in providing, such as working with the elderly, the homeless, and youth. The agency will provide appropriate training.

WALKS/RUNS FOR CHARITABLE ORGANIZATIONS

❑ Multiple Sclerosis Society

117 S. 17th Street
Philadelphia, PA 19103
(215) 963-0100

Comments: There are many Walks and Runs in the Spring and Summer that raise donations for charitable organizations. This is one good example. These walks can be <u>fun</u> and include much socializing before, during and after -- and you'll feel lighter too!

WILDERNESS ACTIVITIES & ENVIRONMENTAL ACTION

❑ Schuylkill Center for Environmental Education

8480 Hagy's Mill Road
Philadelphia, PA
(215) 482-7300

Comments: Volunteers teach nature activities to school children, work in the library, participate in equipment and trail maintenance, etc. Beautiful setting within city limits.

❑ Sierra Club

623 Catharine Street
Philadelphia, PA 19147
(215) 592-4063

Comments: This naturalist group sponsors great outdoor activities (including hiking, bike hikes, boating) and events where you help repair the environment and learn about the issues. Also, they have programs/lectures about natural resources such as a weekend natural history expedition to watch bald eagles. Note: There is a "Singles" subgroup as well!

ZOO

❑ The Philadelphia Zoo

34th Street and Girard Avenue
Philadelphia, PA
(215) 387-6400

Comments: You can be a member of the Zoo which entitles you to help out with a number of fundraising opportunities.

Dancing

BALLROOM
CLASSES
CLASSES & DANCE PARTIES
CONTRA
COUNTRY
COUNTRY - ENGLISH
COUNTRY - WESTERN
FOLK
FOLK - ISRAELI
FOLK, SWING, CONTRA
HIP-HOP AND SOUL
MODERN
POLKA
RAP
ROCK
ROLLER
SCOTTISH
SOBER DANCE
SQUARE
STREET DANCING CLASS
SUFI DANCING
SWING

Folk dancing at the Philadelphia Folk Festival. Courtesy Philadelphia Folk Song Society.

DANCING

DANCING, the universal delight of moving to music, has become for many a performance nightmare instead of the right of spontaneous expression! As the melting pot of many cultures, we seem to have no claim to our <u>own</u> traditional dances. Somehow, we've evolved to where we no longer teach our children to dance, and enjoy dancing at a community level. Instead, in our society, it is thought that DANCING is done only by the graceful, the knowers-of-the-steps, the people who get chosen by partners. "No, I don't dance," is the common refrain at many joyous dancing affairs. I think that means: "I don't dance well," whatever that is. To those who feel this way, I want to suggest that you ask yourself: Do you really want to miss this wonderful activity just because people you don't know (usually) don't like how you do it? The people you <u>do</u> know and who matter to you care only that you are joining them to have fun!

Men and women have danced alone and together since the Very Beginning, probably because, performance aside, it is so much fun, and because it is a first-rate opportunity to have contact with someone you want to get to know better. Probably the best way to get rid of the performance issue is to engage in low-risk dancing events where instruction is provided and where everybody wants to help beginners. Often these DANCING events do not require you to bring a partner. Some are not even partner dances.

Not only is DANCING great fun and interactive, it is also easy to *find.* Networks of dancers abound in the area. There is folk dancing somewhere every night of the week with a rich community of dancers that make up the core group. Try the groups that meet at **Beaver College** (Wednesdays), **Summit Presbyterian Church** (some Thursdays and Saturdays), or **St. Michael's** in Germantown on Friday nights.

There are <u>all kinds</u> of dances for you to learn and become proficient in, from Irish Ceili (**Commodore Barry Club**) and

English Contra (**Summit Church**) to old-fashioned Swing (**That Swing Thing**) and mountain Cajun (**Allons Dancers**). If you want to learn some line dances that are just terrific, try Israeli dancing at most of the YMHA's (**YMHA: Kaiserman Branch**) or Western Country line dancing at a number of Western Country Clubs (**Bronco Bills**) sprinkled throughout the area. You have to be taught to do these dances — they don't just come naturally. That means you have to put effort in to get enjoyment out! The **Mt. Airy Learning Tree** is but one excellent place that offers terrific low cost lessons for all kinds of dances in a comfortable neighborhood atmosphere. Folk dancing, and all its varieties, is foreign to a lot of people. It's really worth exploring, however. I think of it as dancing that is truly user-friendly, and a cross-cultural experience besides!

Then there are the kinds of dances you've always known about and maybe tried a little. These dances are taught throughout the area, and enjoy an enthusiastic following who truly welcome newcomers. Wonderful Ballroom classes are taught at Temple Center City by Paul Wilburn of **Brad Morris Studios** which holds its own classes as well as dance parties! Also, classes and parties are sponsored by the **University City Arts League**, a great place that offers mucho classes in many of the arts. The dance-<u>parties</u> connection is important because if you learn to dance in certain ways, the studio parties offer music that "works," and partners that you know who also learned the same steps you did. When you've become a very experienced dancer, this doesn't matter as much, but in the meanwhile, we strugglers need all the help we can get — because <u>we want to dance now!</u> When you know more about what you're doing, there are a number of fine established ballrooms (**Stardust Ballroom**) in the area, many with live bands and offering instruction of their own before the dance.

How about Square Dancing? The **Tuesday Night Square Dance** in University City has been happening for years and they

will pull you in (gently make room for you) and you, after a million mistakes, will learn. Then YOU are the regular! And Polka — just as there are ballrooms for Ballroom DANCING, so there are ballrooms for Polka, which also include instructions. In fact, there are some places that specifically offer Polka lessons for beginners (**Polish Home Association**). What has *really* taken off in recent years is Country and Western dancing where you can *learn* and *do* the Texas Two-Step all around Philadelphia at places like the **Midnight Rose**.

DANCING is probably happening in your neighborhood more than one night a week, for beginners and advanced dancers, whether you come alone or with a partner. There is dancing for kids, young adults, adults and older adults, in same-age and mixed-age groups. Places to dance can be cheap and informal or elegant and expensive. Churches and synagogues sponsor regular dances, as well as schools, singles' groups, and restaurant/clubs. DANCING IS EVERYWHERE — and always has been since people began. Loving DANCING is our birthright.

People are very sensitive about being pushed to go danc-ing so I want to refrain from this offensive behavior. But if you should just want to look around ... the best places to check are those where instruction is offered and it's likely to be free. People are eager to teach if you show interest, partly because the more people that are enjoying the activity, the more fun the whole group has. You will be valued more for your earnest effort and enthusiasm than for your dance expertise or "cool" exterior. And since partners don't drop out of the sky for any but the gorgeous (And how many of *them* are there?), you might ask someone for one dance to help you learn. Most people are happy to help an eager beginner. On the whole, women are more likely to freely engage in DANCING than men, and commonly decry the lack of men partners. So single men looking for women — consider honing up on your dancing skills!

BALLROOM

❑ Quincy's Sunday Dance

Adam's Mark Hotel
City and Monument Avenues
Philadelphia, PA
(215) 581-5000

Comments: Good dance crowd of all ages where Ballroom dancing is prominently included! Singles and couples here.
Date: Sundays   **Time**: 5-10pm

❑ Stardust Ballroom

Route 73 and Haddonfield Road
Pennsauken, NJ
(609) 663-6376

Comments: A very popular ballroom for Ballroom dancing. Instruction given on Fridays and Saturdays. The group focuses on and practices one dance per month (but they do other dances too!). Single parents dance on Thursdays and Sundays — no partners needed. Occasional Polka parties too!
Date: Friday and Saturday   **Time**: 7:45-12pm
Cost: $5-$5.50
Contact: Russ

❑ Brad Morris DJ and Dance Productions

230 Fairhill Street
Willow Grove, PA
(215) 784-9906

Comments: These dance teachers give dance lessons all over the area — look at the Mt. Airy Learning Tree, Temple University Center City, and Holy Cross College. Dance parties with instruction first are offered in Ballroom and Country-Western so you can use your new dancing talents on a Friday or Saturday night!
Cost: $5 Dance parties

DANCING
Cajun • Ceili

CAJUN

❑ Cajun Dance Party — No Longer
(215) 248-4983

Activity Location: *Brittingham's Irish Pub, 640 Germantown Pike, Lafayette Hill, PA, (215) 828-7351*

Comments: They don't happen anymore, but these were terrific Cajun evenings with Louisiana food, instruction at 5pm and featuring the Schuylkill Bayou Ramblers. Maybe they'll restart if we call and ask for it!

❑ Allons Danser
336 W. Glenside Avenue
Glenside, PA 19038
(215) 576-0839

Activity Location: *Various locations including, Commodore Barry Club, 6815 Emlen Street, Philadelphia PA 19119*

Comments: If you want to learn Cajun dance (It's really neat!) this is a premier group. It organizes most Cajun dancing in the area — including Roxborough, PA, and Arden, DEL. Call for extensive newsletter of events.
Cost: $10 minus $3 if you bring baked goodies

CEILI GROUP

❑ Philadelphia Ceili Group
Commodore Barry Club
6815 Emlen Street
Philadelphia, PA (West Mt. Airy)
(215) 849-8899

Comments: Great Irish music here! Instruction for beginners and dancing for everybody. Festivals in Fall and Spring. Very good group to dance with.
Date: Fridays   **Time**: 8pm
Cost: $10

CLASSES

❑ YMHA — Gershman Branch

Broad and Pine Streets
Philadelphia, PA
(215) 545-4400

Comments: For singles and couples of all ages, reasonably priced classes in Waltz, Swing, Foxtrot, Rumba, Tango. Brush up on your skills or learn from scratch in this Center City location. Ongoing group and your first lesson is free! Bringing partners is not necessary.
Date: Wednesdays   **Time**: 6-9pm
Cost: About $75 for 10 lessons

❑ University Of The Arts - Dance Extension

Broad and Pine Streets
Philadelphia, PA
(215) 875-2269

Comments: Excellent downtown classes in the usual and the unusual types of non-partner dances: Brazilian, Ballet, Jazz, Modern, etc.

CLASSES AND DANCE PARTIES

❑ The Arts League

4226 Spruce Street
Philadelphia, PA
(215) 382-7811

Comments: Located in a large West Philadelphia rowhouse, the League gives classes in Ballroom, Swing and a wide variety of other dances. Then, when you want to dance, they offer Saturday night dance parties with all types of dance music. Come with a partner or meet new dancers!
Date: 1st & 3rd Saturday/month   **Time**: 8:30pm-12am
Cost: $4/Dance parties

❏ Motion Studios

> *7140 Germantown Avenue*
> *Philadelphia, PA (Mt. Airy)*
> *(215) 242-0660*

Comments: This highly diverse program presents all types of dance classes, including Brazilian, African, Swing, Hip Hop and more. Nice atmosphere and high quality instruction. Parking on premises. Call for flyers.

CONTRA

❏ Summit Presbyterian Church

> *Greene and Westview Streets*
> *Philadelphia, PA (Mt. Airy)*
> *(215) 844-3259*

Comments: A period of instruction begins this Contra dancing, although you can get help throughout the evening. Attended by an expert core group and then a number of enthusiastic beginners. Terrific live music and no partner necessary. Saturday dance starts at 8pm.
Date: Thursday & 1st Sat.urday/month   **Time**: 7:30-11pm

COUNTRY

❏ Pineland Country Dancers

> *919 E. Main Street*
> *Maple Shade, NJ 08052*

Activity Location: *Westfield Friends School, Rt.130 and Riverton Road, Cinnaminson, NJ, (609) 779-9084*

Comments: Enthusiastic and welcoming group with small group classes preceding the evening dancing. Excellent for beginners.
Date: Mondays   **Time**: 8-10 pm
Cost: $2.50
Contact: Mae Ann Senior

COUNTRY - ENGLISH

❏ English Country Dancing

Germantown Country Dancers
(215) 247-5993

Activity Location: *Summit Presbyterian Church, Greene and Westview Streets (2nd floor), Philadelphia, PA (West Mt. Airy)*

Comments: A friendly group who will help you through it! Saturdays at Summit, Wednesdays at Calvary Presbyterian Church at Manheim and Pulaski Streets in Germantown. Call for particulars. This dancing is pretty!
Date: 1st Saturday/2nd & 4th Wednesdays **Time**: 8-10:30pm
Cost: $3.50

❏ The Oak English Dancers

Church Of Good Shepherd
3820 The Oak Road
Philadelphia, PA (East Falls)
(215) 844-2474

Comments: Close to Center City, this group offers instruction before dancing.
Date: 1st and 3rd Wednesdays   **Time**: 8-10:30pm

———— COUNTRY - WESTERN

❑ American Cowboy Company

9 Grove Street (At Rte. 70)
Cherry Hill, NJ
(609) 486-0500

Comments: Dance lessons everyday 7-9pm except Sunday (1-6pm and 7-9pm). Music by DJ.
Date: Daily   **Time**: 5pm-3am

❑ Bronco Bills

Grant and Blue Grass Avenues
Philadelphia, PA
(215) 677-8700

Comments: A hopping place with occasional live music. Western theme with a large dance floor. Country dance lessons every night: Monday-Friday instruction at 7:30pm, Saturday instruction from 8-9pm, and Sunday instruction at 1pm includes a brunch! You don't need to come with a partner.
Date: Every night   **Time**: Between 7 and 8:30pm
Cost: $3 weeknights; $5 weekend

❑ Marine Hall

342 Jefferson Street
Bridgeport, PA
(215) 874-0687

Comments: Also on Sundays at 7pm in Wayne, PA, at the United Church Of Christ.
Date: Fridays   **Time**: 7pm
Cost: $5

❏ Midnight Rose Cafe

Routes 309 and 663
Quakertown, PA
(215) 536-3001

Comments: Live music Thursdays, Fridays and Saturdays. Dance lessons Tuesdays through Fridays 7:30-9pm.
Date: All but Mondays   **Time:** 7pm-12 or 1am
Cost: $3 cover/$6 Saturday nights

❏ Y Not Country Dancin'

United Church Of Christ
Walker Road and Route 252
Wayne, PA
(215) 874-0687

Comments: Great Line dancing with instruction for beginners and advanced levels. Line and couple dancing with lessons.
Date: Fridays & Sundays   **Time:** Evenings
Cost: $3- $5
Contact: Tony Bootscooter

FOLK

❏ Pinewoods Camp For Music and Dance

West Long Pond Road
Plymouth, MA 02360
(508) 224-4858

Comments: NOT in Philadelphia, this camp offers a different type of dance, such as Scottish and English Country, Morris, Balkan, etc., every week during the summer. Nationally known teachers provide instruction. Sheer joy I hear — a whole week of dancing!
Cost: Reasonable with scholarships

❏ Eastern Cooperative Recreational School

4711 Chester Avenue
Philadelphia, PA 19143
(215) 729-6738

Activity Location: *Hughesville, PA*
Comments: This group sponsors week-long and weekend camps that include games, storytelling, dance, drama, singing. Lots of great joyous dancing with instruction for beginners. This place is modest and cheap, serves vegetarian food and meets your healthy needs.
  Cost: Very reasonable
Contact: Karen Wisnia

❏ Family Folk Dance

Memorial Church Of Good Shepherd
3820 The Oak Road
Philadelphia, PA (East Falls)
(215) 844-2474

Comments: You can bring the kids to this one — a great activity for the family to do together.
Date: 2nd Sunday/month   **Time:** 2-4:30pm
Cost: $3
Contact: Honey Budnick

❏ Folk Dance Center Of Philadelphia

St. Michael's Lutheran Church
6671 Germantown Avenue
Philadelphia, PA (Mt. Airy)
(215) 624-4242

Comments: I had a great time dancing here, got excellent instruction for all kinds of dances, and all for $3! Beginners warmly encouraged.
Date: Fridays   **Time:** 8-10:30pm

❑ Philadelphia Art Museum (Rocky's Steps)

26th Street and Benjamin Franklin Parkway
Philadelphia, PA
(215) 945-1316

Comments: Folk dancing in front of the Art Museum looking down at the city under the moon has to be one of the most wonderful things to do in Philadelphia. In the winter, dancing used to be in Plaisted Hall; now where? On Monday nights you will be instructed from 7-8pm.

Date: Tuesdays/summer   **Time:** 7pm
     Mondays/winter

Cost: $3

❑ Spring Weekend

Folk Dance Center Of Philadelphia
5806 Greene Street
Philadelphia, PA 19144
(215) 844-3163

Activity Location: *Fellowship Farm*

Comments: Many of the people who dance all year spend this weekend dancing. You can join them even if you're a beginner.

Contact: Bob Simon

❑ Beaver College Folk Dancing Club

Beaver College-Murphy Gym
Easton and Church Roads
Glenside, PA
Day (215-572-2153) Evening (215-233-9399)

Comments: Beaver College has one of the primary weekly dancing events where they welcome and teach beginners. They socialize as well!

Date: Wednesdays   **Time**: 8:15-10:30pm
Cost: $3
Contact: Bill Wadlinger

DANCING
Folk

❏ Westfield Friends Folk Dancers
(215) 457-3706 (local contact)

Activity Location: *Westfield Friends School, Rte.130 and Riverton Road, Cinnaminson, NJ, (609) 893-6138*

Comments: Dancing and instruction for only $3!
Date: 2nd,4th & 5th Friday/month   **Time**: 8-11pm

FOLK - ISRAELI

❏ YMHA - Klein Branch
Cafe Israel
Red Lion and Jamison Roads
Philadelphia, PA (Northeast)
(215) 698-7300

Comments: You don't have to be Jewish to love Israeli dancing! Instruction is provided here and at the Kaiserman Branch at City Line Avenue and Haverford Road (896-7770).
Date: Sundays   **Time**: 7:30-11pm
Cost: $4

❏ YMHA - Gershman Branch
Broad and Pine Streets
Philadelphia, PA
(215) 545-4400

Comments: Instruction provided at this Center City location.
Date: Wednesdays   **Time**: 7-11pm
Cost: $4

DANCING

Folk, Swing, Contra • Hip-Hop and Soul • Modern

FOLK, SWING, CONTRA

❑ Heritage Dance Association

P.O. Box 42415
Philadelphia, PA 19101
(215) 849-5384

Comments: This dance organization sponsors dances on weekends. Many are in Mt. Airy, are cheap, and are well-run with instruction.. They also sponsor a terrific dance festival in fall and spring. Will send fliers of their events.

HIP-HOP AND SOUL

❑ The Ritz

121 South Street
Philadelphia, PA
(215) 925-3042

Comments: No instruction here, but some great music to let loose on!

MODERN

❑ Group Motion

624 S. 4th Street
Philadelphia, PA
(215) 928-1495

Comments: Evenings of Free Style dancing — sort of Modern dance style. You can really express yourself here. No partners needed — you'll make plenty of eye contact once you get there!

DANCING
Polka • Rap • Rock

POLKA

❏ Polish Dance Group
(609) 424-7053

Activity Location*: Polish Home Association, Academy Road,*
Philadelphia, PA, (215) 624-9954

Comments: Polka dance group for young adults. Lessons for beginners every Friday night! People from 16-30's gather for social events and dancing.
Contact: Richard Klimek

RAP

❏ Upper Deck
5708 Germantown Avenue
Philadelphia, PA
(215) 848-0835

Comments: Rap on Sundays, Reggae on Fridays.

ROCK

❏ Waterfront Singles
Eli's Pier 34
Fitzwater Street & Delaware Avenue (S. of Penn's Landing)
Philadelphia, PA
(215) 923-2500

Comments: One of <u>many</u> hot spots with activities along the Delaware River for single young professionals. A dancing and socializing club with periodic activities. Watch the papers for these events.

DANCING
Roller • Scottish

ROLLER

❑ Motion Studios

> 7140 Germantown Avenue
> Philadelphia, PA
> (215) 242-0660

Comments: Roller dance is one of the many innovative programs at Motion. They also offer Tap, Ballet, and Modern as well as unique types of dances like Brazilian, Middle Eastern, and Street Dancing. On Saturdays they sponsor dance parties where you use it! Call for their brochures.

SCOTTISH

❑ Royal Scottish Country Dance Society

> Grace Epiphany Church
> Gowan and Ardleigh Avenues
> Philadelphia, PA 19119 (Chestnut Hill)
> (215) 248-5998

Comments: Great folk dancing group where all ages go to dance. Classes are held in Chestnut Hill, Bryn Mawr, Media and other locations. Also, dance parties take place three times a month along with periodic Highland Balls.
Date: Alternate Fridays
Contact: Geoffrey or Cecily Selling

DANCING
Sober Dance • Square

SOBER DANCE

❑ Sobriety Social Set

> Fiesta Motor Inn-Ballroom
> Rte 611 and PA Turnpike
> Willow Grove, PA
> (215) 663-9107

Comments: This group sponsors dances and fun, sociable evenings for people who want to dance where there is no alcohol.
Date: Saturdays   **Time**: 9pm-1am
Cost: $6

SQUARE

❑ Grand Squares Square Dance Club
> (215)789-7782

Activity Location: *Church Of Holy Comforter, Burmont Road and Bond Avenue, Drexel Hill, PA*

Comments: One of many clubs in the Delaware Valley Square Dancing Federation where some serious square dancing takes place. If you wish to be part of this enjoyable activity, you may take the beginner classes in the Winter. Call Dan for information.
Date: Mondays   **Time**: 8-10pm
Cost: Free

❑ King Squares Square Dancing Club
> (215) 688-5551

Activity Location: *Wayne Senior Center, Across From Penndot Railroad Station,Wayne, PA*

Comments: All ages dance in this very active group. Classes held on Monday nights for serious beginners starting in September. Partners not essential.
Date: Wednesdays   **Time**: 7:30-10pm
Cost: $3 Visitors; $100/year if you join

DANCING

❑ Tuesday Night Square Dance Guild

St. Mary's Parish Hall on Penn Campus
3916 Locust Walk
Philadelphia, PA
(215) 477-8434

Comments: Very popular group has been dancing for years and people love it. No partner or experience needed. Many singles but open to everyone.
Date: 2nd & 4th Tuesdays/month   **Time**: 7:30-10:30pm

STREET DANCING CLASS

❑ Master Street Dance Class

Motion Studios
7140 Germantown Avenue
Philadelphia, PA (Mt. Airy)
(215) 242-0660

Comments: Motion Studios offers standard dancing classes (Tap, Ballet, Modern etc.) as well as current and hip new dances such as this class with great teachers.

SUFI DANCING

❑ Dances Of Universal Peace

83-1 Ferne Boulevard
Drexel Hill, PA 19026
(215) 259-5123

Comments: Sacred dance and spiritual practice dedicated to peace. Rooted in the Sufi tradition, these dances integrate Circle dances and songs from many traditions, including Native American, Judaic, Christian, and others.
Date: Saturdays   **Time**: 8pm
Contact: Jeanne Ayesha Lauenborg

DANCING
Swing

SWING

❑ 20th Century Ballroom

84 S. Lansdowne Avenue
Lansdowne, PA
(215) 465-6479

Comments: Live music by the Good Times and instruction available.
Date: Sundays   **Time**: 8:30pm
Cost: $5

❑ Main Event

Old Lits Building
8th and Market Streets
Philadelphia, PA
(215) 413-1776

Comments: A major place for West Coast Swing. Beginners lesson
starts at 7pm, intermediate lesson about 7:45pm, and open dancing at
8:30pm. This is a great group, often with more men than women!
Date: Mondays and Tuesdays   **Time**: 7pm

❑ Philadelphia Swing Dance Society

(215) 576-0345

Activity Location: *Commodore Barry Club, 6815 Emlen Street,*
Philadelphia, PA

Comments: Large ongoing Swing dance group has been having
dances for years in Mt. Airy. Instruction for beginners 7:30pm. They
will send regular flyers to keep you posted on Swing dance events.
Date: Saturdays   **Time**: 7:30pm-12am
Cost: $5-10

❑ Swing Dance

(215) 576-0345

Activity Location: *Polish Falcons Hall, Salaignac and Terrace Streets, Philadelphia, PA (Manayunk)*

Comments: Jitterbug, Cajun and Country dancing here to the live music by Concrete Canyon Cowpersons. Check the paper for listings of these events.

Date: Many Saturdays   **Time:** 8pm-Midnight

❑ Savoy Dance Club

(215) 542-0463

Activity Location: *Beaver College, Philadelphia, PA*

Comments: Instruction provided. Also held at Gwynedd Mercy College.

Date: Once a month

❑ That Swing Thing

Swing Dance Club
(215) 848-6172

Activity Location: *Calvary Episcopal Church, Pulaski and Manheim Streets, Philadelphia, PA (Germantown)*

Comments: Informal practice sessions to taped music, this dance is not a beginner group. After you take a few instructional dances on other nights, however, you'll fit right in! Call for flyers.

Date: Fridays   **Time:** 8:30-12pm
Cost: $4
Contact: Margaret Fahringer

DISCUSSION GROUPS

ARCHITECTURE
ART
BOOKS
CONTEMPORARY ISSUES
FRENCH LANGUAGE

RECOVERY
SAILING
SOCIAL ACTIVITIES
FOR HIGH IQ'S
WORLD AFFAIRS

DISCUSSION GROUPS

Dinner and discussion of contemporary issues at the White Dog Cafe's "Table Talk."

DISCUSSION GROUPS

Some say we have lost the art of fine conversation and lively discussion, and that many of us are alone with our ideas about literature, politics, spirituality and such. Many complain there is nowhere to go "to talk" nor are there places to discuss things freely and comfortably with a group of thoughtful people, with the further possibility of <u>meeting</u> new people with fresh ideas. Certainly sharing and debating ideas is a wonderful experience and we all need somewhere to exercise the mentally active part of ourselves. We need to use it so we don't lose it!

So *where* can you go for great DISCUSSIONS? One place many people go "to talk" is bars. If you're a comfortable drinker that may work for you, although you also may wish to have discussions on a more serious (and sober) playing field. And, of course, if you are not much of a drinker, bars just don't feel like the right place.

One of the great things about DISCUSSION GROUPS is that they are found in neighborhoods all over the city. Take **Great Books** groups, for example. You can discuss the finest books in the Western World with other thoughtful people in a place pretty close to your house because groups meet in many local areas. The **Free Library** also has interesting lectures/discussions on books and topics related to great reading at your closest branch. (I wonder if we take the Free Library for granted, and don't utilize and value the excellent programs they routinely provide — maybe because it *is* free?)

And, for a short train ride to town, **Borders** presents outstanding presentations/discussions with authors of every kind of book. They also have music events and games and beer tastings and who knows what else. It's FREE — yes, for nothing but your carfare and a great cup of coffee. Borders has started a valuable tradition of integrating a cafe, good books and thoughtful entertainment. Many really enjoy their evenings there. Surely they will offer something of interest to you!

DISCUSSION GROUPS

Forward

If you want a refined evening of dinner and conversation, there is a book group that's been meeting since 1933 (!) called **Bookfriends** which discusses recently published authors. Dinner and good conversation can be had for the modest price of $25. This is an opportunity to meet people who share ideas in an ongoing group.

In the same price range are some terrific programs sponsored by the **White Dog Cafe** in University City. Offered are a "Breakfast Club" and "Table Talk: Food for thought" — evening presentations by sophisticated speakers on all manner of fascinating subjects. White Dog also sponsors theme parties like Bastille Day with coordinated food, dancing and activities.

Another favorite of mine is the lunch time offering by the elegant **Pennsylvania Academy of Fine Arts** — an artist presentation and brown bag discussion at noon for $1.

We must make special mention of the **Utne Reader Salons**, a network of discussion groups established by the magazine *The Utne Reader*. This periodical is interested in idea sharing and it has started a network of serious conversation salons. Each group decides how it will run and what it will talk about. This is a neat idea and has spawned a growing number of Salons in the Philadelphia area. A second Salon tradition sponsored by **Teamworks** has begun at the North Star Bar with monthly **Salon Evenings** for single people. The same organization also sponsors problem-solving discussion groups related to personal goals.

Who is going to be in these groups? Intimidating people? Maybe. People who know a lot about the subject, or at least know more than you (or think they do!), and therefore make you feel stupid? As if they are thinking: "What is HE doing here?" Maybe.

There certainly are people like that in what would seem to be nice places, who, for their own reasons, need to behave in a patronizing way. You can let them be the gatekeepers to the world you want to explore (or you worry in advance that THEY might be there) — OR you can decide that you'll be in charge of where you go and what you learn and discuss, thank you very much, and if they're so distressed that you don't know "anything," THEY can leave. This, of course, does not mean that you want to go barging about, dominating the time with beginner questions, etc. But I know you wouldn't do that. You'd watch for a while, get a feel for the place and the group norms, and venture in with some consideration for your own newness. And when you're ready, you <u>will</u> put in your two cents and begin to be <u>part of the group</u> — probably a valued member at that!

Whom will you meet? You will certainly meet people who are interested in things, want to learn, want to bat ideas around to further their own thinking, and want to have their ideas on the table for reaction. You'll meet people who do not want to spend their lives watching TV, who prefer being in an active rather than passive mode. After all, they got <u>there</u> didn't they? And they probably enjoy interaction with people, which is why they are out there interacting — the way <u>YOU</u> are!

For the Resisters ("I'd like to try a new group but..."): I think that to get yourself to venture out you may need to give yourself permission (as we psychologists like to say) NOT to say anything if you don't feel like it. But do remember: You don't have to *know* anything about a subject to want to learn about it or ask questions. Once you've started, you may find that a world opens up to you.

On the other hand, if you go, you might find out that you *don't* enjoy the subject, even though you thought you might. Having gone to check it out means you concluded this after a fair chance.

If you <u>never</u> feel "in the right mood" to risk a new group, let me encourage you to GO anyway and check one out because

where you are

what you are doing

and what you are talking about   can change your life.

DISCUSSION GROUPS

Architecture • Art • Books

ARCHITECTURE

❑ Foundation For Architecture

Shops At Liberty Place
16th & Market Streets
Philadelphia, PA
(215) 569-3187

Comments: A special series of lectures about the beautiful and historical buildings of Philadelphia that usually runs about two months, one evening a week.
Date: January-April
Cost: Free

ART

❑ Art At Lunch

Pennsylvania Academy Of Fine Arts
Broad & Cherry Streets
Philadelphia, PA
(215) 972-7600

Comments: Now <u>this</u> is a great deal! Bring your own lunch and engage in informal talks, discussions and artist demonstrations, often related to the current exhibit. The Academy also sponsors dialogues with artists ("Artist Consultations") on specified afternoons. Call about receiving fliers.
Date: First Wed/month   **Time:** Noon
Cost: $1.50 includes coffee!

BOOKS

❑ Northeast Regional Library

2228 Cottman Avenue
Philadelphia, PA
(215) 685-0515

Comments: Reading and discussion groups at this branch of the Free Library include such topics as: "Worlds to Discover — the Immigrant Experience." Books needed are made available at the library. Check your local library for its events.

DISCUSSION GROUPS

Books

❑ Bookfriends Association of Philadelphia

19 E. Dartmouth Circle
Media, PA 19063
(215) 743-1690

Activity Location: *Various restaurants in the area.*

Comments: This interesting group is about 25 years old and holds three dinner meetings a year with talk/discussions by recently published authors.
Cost: About $25 for dinner and discussion
Contact: Dorothy F. Lawley

❑ Borders Book Shop

1727 Walnut Street
Philadelphia, PA
(215) 568-7400

Comments: You probably know that almost *every* night Borders has terrific talks and presentations about books, games, and contemporary issues of interest. Afterwards, you can hang around, drink coffee and continue the discussion! Check the Borders in Chestnut Hill, Rosemont and Cherry Hill for great programs as well.
Time: 7:30pm
Cost: Free

❑ Great Books Program

Philadelphia, PA
(215) 732-8727

Activity Location: *Various locations in the area*

Comments: These pithy discussions on Homer, Chaucer, Machiavelli, Tolstoy and others may be taking place right around the corner from your house! People who go love these groups.
Cost: Free
Contact: Joe Blume

DISCUSSION GROUPS

❑ Mystery Book Club

Barnes & Noble Bookstore
720-730 Lancaster Avenue
Bryn Mawr, Pa 19010
(215) 520-0355

Comments: A book club that discusses British, American and award-winning mystery authors who read for the group. They also read and discuss books from a reading list and mystery book journal. Writers and readers welcome!
Date: 2nd Wednesday/month   **Time:** 7:30-8:30pm

❑ Moonstone Readings

Robin's Book Store
108 S. 13th Street
Philadelphia, PA
(215) 735-9600

Comments: Well known authors read from and discuss their works. Moonstone also sponsors conferences featuring certain author groups such as women writers, black writers, etc.

❑ "Calling All Fiction Lovers"

Temple University Center City (TUCC)
1616 Walnut Street
Philadelphia, PA
(215) 204-6946

Comments: This course is typical of the kinds of discussion courses given by Temple Center City. Check the catalog for other great subjects!
Date: Mondays (8)   **Time:** 7:30-9:20pm
Cost: About $125/course

—————— CONTEMPORARY ISSUES

❏ Tight Wad Exchange

> *Arnold's Way*
> *Main Street in Manayunk*
> *Philadelphia, PA*
> *(215) 483-2266*

Comments: Individuals interested in sharing information (*Hot Tips!*) about frugal living get together. Lots of intriguing group discussions and workshops take place at Arnold's Way.

❏ Serving Food With Thought

> *White Dog Cafe*
> *3420 Sansom Street*
> *Philadelphia, PA*
> *(215) 386-9224*

Comments: White Dog sponsors regular speakers and group discussion dinner events that focus on interesting current topics. Other programs include "Table Talk" where people interested in the topic listen to a great speaker (e.g., in 7/94: *Inquirer* journalists Bartlett and Steele!) and eat one of those terrific White Dog dinners. Get on their mailing list — these evenings are top notch!

❏ Ellen Rose Restaurant

> *5920 Greene Street*
> *Philadelphia, PA (Germantown)*
> *(215) 843-1525*

Comments: This charming spot with good food and informal ambiance has occasional discussion nights on art, literature, music, and travel. Interest in these evenings ebbs and flows so be sure to call about it; you may even encourage a few topic groups yourself!

DISCUSSION GROUPS

❏ Encore Books

Commerce Square
20th & Market Streets
Philadelphia, PA
(215) 735-6991

Comments: Encore sponsors reading and discussion "Forums" on topics like environmental issues, banking, finance, real estate, health care and others.
Date: 1st Wednesday/month
Contact: Lauren Stevenson

❏ Free Library Of Philadelphia

(215) 686-5322

Comments: Books aside, the Free Library has talks on many subjects such as quilting, Thailand, career searching, various films, etc. These interesting discussions are happening all the time in many branches, usually to rather small and comfortable audiences.
Cost: Free

❏ Philadelphia Ethical Society

1906 S. Rittenhouse Square
Philadelphia, PA 19103
(215) 735-3456

Comments: This organization provides opportunities for discussions on all types of issues that relate to our values and humanistic principles. Examples of the Sunday topics: "A Bicycler's View Of Humanity;" and "The Puerto Rican Community: Past-Present-Future." Stop in and pick up literature describing upcoming presentations.

DISCUSSION GROUPS

❏ Salon Evenings

Teamworks
P.O. Box 15854
Philadelphia, PA 19103
(215) 545-7259

Activity Location: *North Star Bar, 27th & Poplar Streets, Philadelphia, PA*

Comments: These evenings take place periodically in various locations where people gather to hear presentations and discuss topics like "What's love anyway?" and "Great places to meet people." (by guess who??) Good conversations and networking happen here!
Date: Sundays once a month   **Time:** 5:30-8:30pm
Cost: $35 includes dinner
Contact: Phyllis Mufson

❏ Friday Forums

Temple Association For Retired Professionals (TARP)
Temple University Center City
1619 Walnut Street
Philadelphia, PA
(215) 787-1505

Comments: Great programs for retired people who want to stay current and who enjoy good discussions. Fall of 1993 programs included speakers such as Judge Lisa Richette, Chamber of Commerce President Charles Pizzi and Richard Breslin, president of Drexel University.
Date: Fridays   **Time:** 10:30am

DISCUSSION GROUPS

❏ Lunchtime Learning

> *Temple University Center City*
> *1616 Walnut Street*
> *Philadelphia, PA 19103*
> *(215) 787-1619*

Comments: First-rate short classes and discussions given over lunch (you bring) for busy Center City professionals on practical and business-related topics.

Date: Wednesdays **Time**: 12:30-1:30pm
Cost: $10

❏ First Friday Coffee Group

> *Unitarian Society Of Germantown*
> *6511 Lincoln Drive*
> *Philadelphia, PA 19119*
> *(215) 844-1157*

Comments: The Unitarian Society hosts many types of discussions about books, poetry and contemporary issues. They also have coffee and conversation before the Sunday service.

Date: 1st Friday/month **Time:** 10am

❏ Salons For Conversation

> *Utne Reader Magazine*
> *pick up at the newsstand*

Comments: This magazine, that deals with current topics, has started conversational salons based on the 18th century salons where people engaged in great talk! Send them your name and money and they'll provide an address for you to find the Utne Salon in your area.

Cost: $12 to join

DISCUSSION GROUPS

French Language • Recovery • Sailing

FRENCH LANGUAGE

❑ French Table Monthly Meeting

Alliance Francaise
1420 Walnut Street; Suite 1202
Philadelphia, PA
(215) 735-5283

Activity Location: *Cosmopolitan Club, 1616 Latimer Street, Philadelphia, PA*

Comments: Numerous events both in French and/or about France, including: receptions, concerts, lectures, presentations, discussions, classes, tours, travel, library, Cine-club are offered.
Date: Monthly   **Time:** Noon

RECOVERY

❑ Starting Point

Haddonfield, NJ
(609) 854-3155

Activity Location: *Various locations in the area*

Comments: Program offering lectures and informal discussions for people interested in recovery from addictions. Series include Adult Children Of Alcoholics, Co-Dependency Series, 12-Step Series, and more.
Date: Sundays   **Time:** 7:30-8:30pm

SAILING

❑ Philadelphia Maritime Museum

Converted Barge On Penn's Landing
321 Chestnut Street
Philadelphia, PA
(215) 925-5439

Comments: Lectures and activities at the museum, such as "Adventures of Yachting." Also workshops on the water have included: "Boatbuilding Demystified," and "Oar Making, and Sail Making."
Cost: $7/$5 For talks; between $50 and $200 for classes

DISCUSSION GROUPS

SOCIAL ACTIVITIES FOR HIGH IQ'S

❏ Mensa

Friend's Meeting House
4th & Arch Streets
Philadelphia, PA
(215) 765-2735 Hotline of Activities

Comments: Monthly meetings of this group held here. This highly intelligent group also meets for luncheons, dinners, meetings and speakers, weekend outings, sailing and after-work get-togethers. Admission test required to join.
Date: 2nd Friday/month
Cost: Membership $30/year

WORLD AFFAIRS

❏ Circle Of Reason (& Other Programs)

International House
3701 Chestnut Street
Philadelphia, PA 19104
(215) 387-5125

Comments: This institution is devoted to promoting cross-cultural understanding and sponsors cultural exchanges. Enjoy concerts and films and be part of workshops and discussions with people from other countries.
Cost: $30/year

❏ World Affairs Council Of Philadelphia

1314 Chestnut Street
Philadelphia, PA
(215) 563-5363

Comments: This thoughtful group sponsors informative dinners, discussions, lectures, seminars, tours, exhibits and films. They also have a subgroup for people in their 20's and 30's.

DISCUSSION GROUPS

— NOTES —

CLASSES
CLASSIC & CULTURAL FILMS
TRAVEL
UNUSUAL
VIDEO MAKING

FILMS

Screening of "Alma's Rainbows" at the Philadelphia Festival of World Cinema, May 1993.

FILMS

Going to the movies is one of the most popular social activities in America. It is definitely something we do with others, but unless you're 13 and going to a Saturday afternoon matinee, you're not likely to meet new people at a regular movie house.

Since this is a book about connecting with *new* people, the listing here only includes movies where there is some kind of planned interaction included, like a post-film discussion, or where interaction is very likely to happen, such as at showings of unusual films with receptions, where you feel "like" the other people who would be there. In these kinds of situations, the type of movie tells you something about the interests of the people attending, especially if you see them at that type of movie on a regular basis. David Grossman says that he has a regular following at his **Film Forum** of unusually fine classic FILMS shown every Saturday night. He also mentioned that some viewers commonly go out for coffee following the films. By the way, the day I talked to David he was about to show the first Italian talkie which he had been trying to get from film archives for over two years; he said it was astonishingly beautiful.

Personally, I would really like to see more of the CINE CAFES like those held during **Philadelphia's International Film Festival**. The CAFES had informative guided discussions which gave people opportunities to have good conversations with others — not just the friends they came with — about the film experience they'd just had. It's a great way to meet and talk with interesting people who might share your cinematic preferences!

Actually, with some notable exceptions, Philadelphia is only beginning to develop as a good FILM city. This makes the loss of **Temple's Cinemathetique** outstanding weekly movies all the greater. On the up-side, however, besides the aforemen-

tioned **Film Forum**, there are several excellent classic and cultural FILM activities. Very special mention must be made of the **Philadelphia International Film Festival** held every May at International House and at local movie houses throughout the city. Not only is this an extraordinary event with a wide variety of wonderful FILMS from famous and local film makers, but also it attracts a wide diversity of people who go to see them. It is not to be missed! Also sponsored by **International House** is the **Neighborhood Film/Video Project**, a collection of events including a weekly venue of outstanding international cinema. You can find them listed weekly in the *Daily News'* "Weekend" section. These showings are sometimes accompanied by a talk and guided discussion. (If we all request this, they are more likely to schedule it.) **Villanova** also shows classic FILMS which includes an expert to field questions and discussion, and so do various branches of the **Free Library** where the FILMS are free.

Looking for specialized FILMS? The **Art Museum** combines workshops and films about art and artists (e.g., "The Impressionists") on Saturdays. FILMS about travel and magnificent geographical documentaries are shown by the **Geographical Society** where you can meet the people who photographed them and lived them! Special cultural FILM programs can be found in their related institutions (e.g., Jewish history at the **Gershwin YMHA**). Call these and other institutions for information about the programs they present on a regular basis — often to woefully small but very interested audiences. These kinds of programs are usually informal and conversational — and the people who go are <u>interested</u> and <u>interesting</u>.

One of my favorites is **bizarre films by Todd** which used to be shown at **Silk City** on Spring Garden Street and are now playing at **Borders** on a somewhat regular basis. This has imagination and sounds like fun! You can call Borders to find out the schedule. Similarly, the **Khyber Pass** has something called **Secret Cinema**. You have to check that one out yourself!

For the shyest interactors, going to FILM events is one of the easiest things to try. It's not too hard to go to the movies and if you get nervous about joining the discussion, you can simply go home after the movie or just listen. It might be hard to go alone, but try it. Once you get used to it it's kind of neat, because you can go on the spur of the moment, even when you're supposed to be doing your bills or weekly laundry. Also, you don't have to find someone who is in the same mood you're in to see what you feel like seeing. It's a luxury to go alone — and once you're there you might be more inclined to take a risk, chat with the person next to you, and even give YOUR opinion in the discussion!

CLASSES

❏ Temple University Center City

1616 Walnut Street
Philadelphia, PA 19103
(215) 204-4335

Comments: TUCC offers an introductory class in photography and darkroom activity for the budding photographer.

❏ The University City Arts League

4226 Spruce Street
Philadelphia, PA 19104
(215) 382-7811

Comments: The League offers several classes in photography including this one: "Basic Black and White Photography."

CLASSIC & CULTURAL FILMS

❏ Film Forum

Philadelphia Senior Center
509 S. Broad Street
Philadelphia, PA 19147
(215) 732-7704

Comments: Specialty films from outstanding film collections brought to Philadelphia by film expert David Grossman. Some go for coffee afterwards to discuss the films.
Date: Saturdays   **Time**: 7pm
Cost: FF Membership $10

❑ Free Library Of Philadelphia

Montgomery Auditorum, Central Branch
Logan Square on Vine Street
Philadelphia, PA
(215) 686-5322

Comments: Classic movies shown to you for free. A calendar listing films to be shown is available at all city branches.
Date: Sundays: 2pm; Tuesdays: 7pm
Cost: Free

❑ Philadelphia Festival Of World Cinema

International House of Philadelphia
3701 Chestnut Street
Philadelphia, PA
(215) 895-6593

Comments: For two short weeks in May, a fabulous collection of films is shown, featuring both internationally famous filmmakers (e.g., Lina Wertmueller), and fine local filmmakers such as Eugene Martin. Engage in guided film talks over coffee at associated Cine Cafes at places like Borders and the Last Drop Cafe.
Date: Every night for two weeks in May
Cost: About $6 for one evening

❑ Philadelphia Museum Of Art

Van Pelt Auditorium
26 Street & Benjamin Franklin Parkway
Philadelphia, PA
(215) 763-8100

Comments: Excellent film programs about art and artists.
Date: Weekends

❑ Neighborhood Film/Video Project

International House
3701 Chestnut Street
Philadelpha, PA 19104
(215) 895-6542

Comments: Tons of films: videos from Lincoln Center Film Society, unusual prints of classic films, and little shown films by excellent film makers. University teachers lead discussions. Also, several workshops for media artists and more.

❑ Villanova University

Connelly Center
Villanova, PA
(215) 645-4750

Comments: In their Culture Film Festival, most films feature guest speakers and discussions following film presentations. Call for newsletter of upcoming films.

DISABLED CULTURAL FILMS

❑ Neighborhood Film/Video Project

Creative Access at International House
3701 Chestnut Street
Philadelphia, PA 19104
(215) 895-6542

Comments: This group provides subtitles on <u>current</u> English language films such as "Jurassic Park" and "The Firm" (Spring '94). The aim is to provide accessibility of these films to deaf people in the Philadelphia area.

DISCUSSION GROUPS

❑ **Penn State University - Integrative**

> *YMHA — Gershman Branch*
> *Broad and Pine Streets*
> *Philadelphia, PA*
> *(215) 545-4400*

Comments: A series of current movie topic discussions.
Date: Thursdays   **Time**: 11am

TRAVEL/ADVENTURE FILMS - NARRATION

❑ **The Geographical Society of Philadelphia**

> *21 South 12th Street, Suite 909*
> *Philadelphia, PA 19107*

Activity Location:*Academy of Music, Broad & Locust Streets, Philadelphia, PA, (215) 563-0127*

Comments: Films of amazing and beautiful places shown weekly. This organization takes trips, sponsors programs and has a great library.
Date: Weds (October-April)   **Time:** 7:45pm
Cost: Non-members - $7.00. $50/Yr. Membership

UNUSUAL FILMS

❏ Todd's Found Films

Border's Book Store
1727 Walnut Street
Philadelphia, PA
(215) 568-7400

Comments: Yes — Todd's Back! This was a "No Longer" Entry but Todd has reappeared at Borders showing his "Bizarre Films" which he has resurrected. Call about it!
Date: Tuesdays   **Time**: 9pm
Cost: Free

VIDEO MAKING

❏ Scribe Video Center

Video Makers' Workign Group
1342 Cypress Street
Philadelphia, PA
(215) 735-3785

Comments: Offers Videography Classes, including: The Media and The Truth (Screening & Discussion Workshop), Scriptwriting and others.

Games, Sports & Outdoors

BIKING

BOATING - CANOEING

BOATING - ROWING

BOATING - SAILING

**BOATING - SAILING
FOR WOMEN**

BOATING - WHITEWATER RAFTING

FISHING

GAMES - ADULT GAMES

BOARD GAMES

GOLF

GROUPS FOR RECREATION

HIKING

NATURE

RACEWALKING CLUB

RUNNING

TENNIS

MISCELLANY

GAMES, SPORTS & OUTDOORS

White-water rafting on the Lehigh River with Dynamic Diversions.

Enjoyment at the Philadelphia Folk Festival. Photo by Dan Peck, Riverside Photo.

GAMES, SPORTS & OUTDOORS
Forward

As you move through this section, you will see but a sample of the wonderful interactive physical activities that Philadelphia and environs has to offer. If you are interested in staying trim and lowering your stress level while having fun at the same time, then this is the chapter for you. Another great advantage in partaking in these activities is that you will not meet any couch potatoes there. The people you will find care enough about themselves to get moving and be involved in life and most likely they enjoy fun and laughter while doing it! (On the other hand, I'm trying to remember the last time I had fun and laughter over my golf game...!) Those are pretty neat people to spend time with, don't you think? They'll think that about you too!

Honestly, I am <u>astounded</u> at the great diversity of activities to be found in the Philadelphia area where you can **play** at something — whether a physical sport or a game of mental strategy. You find everything from the **Exton SCRABBLE Club** (where you can learn to play tournament SCRABBLE) to **Gazela**, probably the activity most dear to my heart in this whole book. Ever hear of Gazela? It is the oldest, largest, wooden sailing ship that is still sailing in the world. Guess where it is? Here, at Penn's Landing in <u>Philadelphia</u>. What does it cost you to tour her? A donation as little as 50 cents is requested, but please give more to this local treasure owned by the **Philadelphia Ship Preservation Guild.** And if you wanted to participate in the activities that keep her alive, *if you wanted to sail her just like the Portuguese sailors over 100 years ago,* what would it cost you? Can you imagine that it costs a pittance (about $50) to belong because this is a volunteer crew and all sail training is provided on-board the ship. If you are willing to help maintain her by doing such things as painting, sewing sails, carpentry, etc., you can be on the crew that sails her to places like Nova Scotia or Virginia Beach in the summers. And who will you meet on the Gazela? People who love sailing, who love history, who love sea chanties, and who are not afraid of dedicated work.

Now, maybe this isn't your cup of tea. If swabbing a deck or learning the names of fore and aft sails isn't your idea of a good time (although I can't believe it — I *loved* being on the crew), then the Gazela is not for you. Then how about a great game of Walleyball with **Dynamic Diversions**, a local recreational group that sponsors many different types of outdoor fun activities. These include skiing and sailing as well as road rallies (a team scavenger hunt in cars), parties at the River Club in Manayunk, and more. Or how about learning to play billiards (**River City Billiards**) or backgammon, joining a bowling league (**at Erie Lanes**) or flying a kite on Belmont Plateau (**Annual Kite Flying Festival**)? There are lots of great groups to take hikes with, some of which focus on a particular topic like birds or flowers (**Schuylkill Center for Environmental Education**), or historical trail exploration (American **Youth Hostels**), and some who hike just for the sheer joy of it. One hiking group which I just took real notice of is the **Wanderlust** group, sponsored by the City's Department of Recreation, which takes hike-walks all over the city. These are not killer hikes; you don't need L.L. Bean shoes for these hikes. Just a lively, curious spirit and a reasonably well working body. There are lots of nice people hiking on Saturdays and Sundays around here.

One of the things you will notice about the activities listed in this chapter is that most of them are low cost or free. Secondly, you can see that they are distributed all over the city. There are places to play *everywhere!* And these events take place on many days of the week and at many times of day. If you want to get out for it, it's out there for you!

A Note for people who feel nervous about the idea of PLAYING — "At **your** age"
          — "At your **weight**"   (or better yet —)

— "Isn't it sort of **immature**...?"

    <u>My personal Response</u>: To many people, GAMES, SPORTS & OUTDOORS are the quintessential activities to do when you want to have fun. To them, GAMES & SPORTS define what is meant by "leisure time."
    This may not be true for you — but can we talk about that? Lots of times people think that all games and sports are very rigorous, appropriate only for the most hale and hearty. Also, they think that GAMES & SPORTS require a keen competitive spirit — maybe even a sort of crushing mean streak. Women especially seem to see sports as primarily the province of men engaging in some kind of macho power games.

    Even if this is sort-of what you think:
    Please do not eliminate this section from your perusal.
    I think you may be surprised at some of the listings. Actually, you may be surprised at <u>your interest</u> in some of the possibilities for you to expand and try something different.
    Think about these things.
    Mull them over, and **then** make up your own mind...

AND NOW ——— <u>HERE'S A SNEAK PREVIEW!</u>

    <u>BIKING</u>: You could buy *Short Bike Rides in Eastern Pennsylvania* (by Bill Simpson) and try some terrific local paths to see if you're in shape, or you could go right out and meet with the **Bicycle Club of Philadelphia** on Sundays at noon on Boat House Row for its beginner or advanced bike trips. Nice folks, and they watch out for you the first few times. Tell them you're new.

    <u>BOATING</u>: There's so much water around here: Lake Nockamixon and Marsh Creek, the Schuylkill and Delaware Rivers, Wissahickon Creek, and the Atlantic Ocean! These

waters allow for all <u>kinds</u> of boating for all levels of boating skill. Can you imagine kayaking along the upper Schuylkill, or sail-racing on the Delaware some evening after work (**Liberty Yacht Club**), learning about small wooden boats (**Traditional Small Craft Association**), or even dipping into celestial navigation (pun intended)! There aren't many more effective stress reducing situations than listening to the water lapping on the sides of your gently rocking boat as you anchor at sunset — and it can be found, *abundantly found*, right here in Philadelphia!

<u>GAMES</u>: People drive from as far as Reading and Wilmington every Monday to play SCRABBLE with the **Exton SCRABBLE Club**. My take on this group is that they are pretty serious SCRABBLE players, although they have an excellent social time as well. I *hate* SCRABBLE, regularly dump the board on my partner's lap, so this activity is not for me. But conversation with members of this group convince me that <u>they</u> really enjoy this game, and each other! They welcome beginners, so you don't have to be a crackerjack player to start in their group — just enthusiastic and willing to learn.

If you want to play games that are not very competitive, that have easygoing, pleasurable fun as the main objective, try the **Eastern Cooperative Recreational School** programs. Some of the best games leaders in the area will lead you in the most enjoyable games-activities you can remember. In fact, many of them will remind you of the imaginative games you played as a kid. Call them — that's not the only thing they have fun doing!

By the way, please find chess, checkers, bridge and other games included in the chapter on HOBBIES & CLUBS.

<u>GOLF</u>: Golf is everywhere these days — for *all* of us, not just rich people. Check out the city's public courses. Walnut Lane is delightful, pretty and green, challenging, and not real long. Women are taking it pretty seriously too these days,

presenting a serious challenge to the guys (*heh, heh*). In fact, the **Executive Women's Golf League** offers an opportunity for women to meet other women to play golf with and network around other interests as well.

GROUPS FOR RECREATION: One of the nice things about joining recreational groups is that you can meet a bunch of people who, because they like to be active, partake in a variety of engaging events. **Dynamic Diversions** is a club that meets regularly to take part in many invigorating events such as mountain hiking, Chesapeake Bay sailing, billiards, ice skating and parties! They have a terrific agenda, and will send you a newsletter to prepare you for up-coming events.

HIKING: You can hike short or you can hike long. You can hike in the area or you can hike on mountain tops. You can be as skilled as major HikerWoman or you can be an ordinary business person who likes to just walk around and look at things. You will meet a wide variety of people doing this, many of them with detailed knowledge about different areas of nature, architecture and geography. That doesn't mean you have to be knowledgeable yourself; after all, they need people to listen! And, of course, a side benefit of hiking-walking is lost pounds, roses in your cheeks and an exhilarating experience...

RUNNERS/SKIERS/TENNIS NUTS: You know who you are, but did you know how many groups there were to connect with?

MISCELLANY: This section was the *most fun to compile.* Just LOOK at what you can do around here! You can play tiny billiards and take lessons in drink- and smoke-free regular size billiard halls. You can run around and play frisbee, frisbee golf and fly kites. You can play volleyball and you can rock-climb. There are people to play horseshoes with or to join for horse-

back riding. Also martial arts, racewalking, fencing, synchronized swimming, archery and volleyball.

And more.

All around here.

All with groups who may be established and are delighted
to have new members, or with people who come together for a
day or two to participate in a new thing.

You can go with a friend, or you can go alone and make
friends. You really can.

BIKING

❑ Bicycle Club Of Philadelphia

P.O. Box 30235
Philadelphia, PA 19103
(215) 440-9983

Activity Location: *#1 Boat House, Boat House Row on Kelly Drive, Philadelphia, PA*

Comments: Premier recreational bike group in Philadelphia, this group sponsors rides for various levels of riders (15-100 miles) on Sundays around noon. They also have Sunday morning breakfast rides! All rides led by experienced leaders and you don't have to be a member to ride. Newsletter listing events.

Date: Sundays   **Time:** Mornings
Cost: $15 Membership

❑ Bicycle Coalition Of Delaware Valley

P.O. Box 8194
Philadelphia, PA 19101
215-BIC-YCLE

Comments: Group members advocate the bicycle as important means of transportation as well as a recreational activity. They hold meetings, sponsor events, and put out an interesting newsletter.

❑ Suburban Cyclists Unlimited

P.O. Box 401
Horsham, PA 19044
(215) 675-1174

Activity Location: *Horsham Township Building, Horsham Road, Horsham, PA*

Comments: This group enjoys a variety of trips and races out there in the beautiful Philadelphia 'burbs. They also hold meetings and sponsor social events. Newsletter available.

Date: 1st Thursday/month   **Time**: 8pm
Contact: Joe Serrotone

GAMES, SPORTS & OUTDOORS

❏ Wissahickon Off-Road Cyclists

(215) 271-7325

Activity Location: *Valley Green Inn in Fairmount Park, Philadelphia, PA*

Comments: This responsible biking group that rides in the Wissahickon is committed to preserving the beauty of the Wissahickon Valley. They sponsor regular trail maintenance events as well as help park rangers doing trail patrol.

Date: 3rd Sunday/month   **Time**: 11:30am

BOATING - CANOEING

❏ Philadelphia Canoe Club

4900 Ridge Avenue
Philadelphia, PA (Lower Roxborough)
(215) 828-0760

Comments: You can learn to canoe and kayak with this group. They hold an annual fun day with an open house and a regatta.
Cost: Free
Contact: Bob McNamara

BOATING - ROWING

❏ Novice Rowing Classes

Bachelors Barge on Boathouse Row
6 Kelly Drive
Philadelphia, PA
(215) 769-9335

Comments: 300 members participate in competitive and recreational rowing for men and women of all ages.
Date: Summer

GAMES, SPORTS & OUTDOORS

❑ Crescent Boat Club

Boathouse Row
5 Kelly Drive
Philadelphia, PA
(215) 978-9816

Comments: 40 members enjoy competitive and recreational rowing and sculling for men and women of all ages.

❑ Upper Merion Boat Club

738 Hidden Valley Road
King of Prussia, PA 19406
(215) 337-3624

Activity Location: *North Front Street, Bridgeport, PA*

Comments: 110 men and women members do competitive and recreational rowing and sculling with free lessons for beginners. Rowing program available for people with disabilities. Canoeing is available here too.
Cost: Adults: $100/ Students: $75
Contact: Tom Pappanastasiou

BOATING - SAILING

❑ Sailing Classes

Annapolis Sailing School
P.O. Box 3334
Annapolis, MD 21403
(800) 638-9192

Activity Location: *Severn River in Annapolis on the Chesapeake Bay*

Comments: Well-known sailing school nearby provides weekend beginner and advanced classes sailing on 24' rainbow sloops. Learn basic sailing skills and navigation in indoor and "wet" classes.
Cost: About $400 per weekend

GAMES, SPORTS & OUTDOORS

Boating - Sailing

❑ Annual Constitution Cup Regatta

Philadelphia Maritime Museum
(215) 925-5439

Activity Location: *Corinthian Yacht Club, Delaware River, Essington, PA*

Comments: Watch or crew in races of traditional (late 19th Century) small pleasure craft right outside Philadelphia. Great fun!

❑ Liberty Sailing School & Yacht Club

Penn's Landing Area
235 North Columbus Boulevard, Pier 12
Philadelphia, PA 19106
(215) 922-4005

Comments: This club offers sailing and racing on the Delaware River almost every night with other people who love sailing! Also lectures, slides, trips, classes and great social events.
Cost: Memberships between $650 and up
Contact: Peter McGowan, General Manager

❑ Philadelphia Sailing Club

Germantown Cricket Club
Manheim Street off Wissahickon Avenue
Philadelphia, PA (Germantown)
(215) 668-1234 (Hotline)

Comments: Major Philadelphia sailing group for men and women, beginners and experts, who sail nearby and go on sailing vacations. Monthly meetings are fun.
Date: 3rd Wednesday/month   **Time:** 8pm
Cost: Reasonable

❑ Gazela Of Philadelphia

Philadelphia Ship Preservation Guild
Penn's Landing
Delaware Avenue & Chestnut Street
Philadelphia, PA 19106
(215) 923-9030

Comments: Be part of a volunteer crew that maintains and sails this historic tall ship. Sail-training classes on board teach you how to sail a square rigger so <u>you</u> can be a part of this group that sails to Boston, Nova Scotia, Norfolk and New York! Enthusiastic novices welcome.
Date: All year
Cost: Less than $70 for uniform and insurance

❑ Traditional Small Craft Association

Workshop On The Water ("The Barge")
Penn's Landing On Delaware Avenue
Philadelphia , PA

Comments: Terrific small craft sailing club for those interested in classic, often wooden, boats. Monthly meetings offer speakers, trips, slides, and sailing on the Delaware River.
Cost: About $35

❑ Sailing Classes

U.S. Coast Guard Auxiliary
(215) 789-0114

Activity Location: *Various locations in Philadelphia*

Comments: Basic training classes covering all aspects of boating skills and information. Navigation, knots, sailing techniques, safety information — the works! Taught by seasoned sailors and attended by enthusiastic learners.
Cost: About $35 includes materials
Contact: Muriel Lewis

BOATING - SAILING FOR WOMEN

❑ Womanship

410 Severn Avenue
Annapolis, MD 21403
(800) 342-9295

Activity Locations: *Various locations — Annapolis, MD, Newport, RI, Florida, and the Caribbean.*

Comments: Great organization for women to learn sailing in the company of other women. The gorgeous Chesapeake Bay is the local setting for these classes.

BOATING - WHITE WATER RAFTING

❑ Pocono White Water Adventures

America's Rafting Center
Route 903
Jim Thorpe, PA 18229
(717) 325-3656

Comments: A premier white water rafting group for beginners and advanced rafters. You can go with friends or alone and they will put you in a raft with other adventurers!
Date: Mid March-Mid November   **Time**: 4-6 hours/trip
Cost: About $35 for day trip

FISHING

❑ Main Line Fly-Tyers Club

654 Easton Road
Glenside, PA
(215) 885-0917

Activity Location: *St. Peter's Episcopal Church, Glenside, PA*

Comments: This group of men and women (Yes, women fish too!) meet to hear top fishing speakers, discuss great places to fish, and find out the best ways to catch them. They have beginner and advanced classes, and then use these skills on group fishing trips.
Cost: $25/year to join
Contact: Dick Baker

GAMES - ADULT GAMES

❑ Playful Community

Omega
260 Lake Drive
Rhinebeck NY 12572
(914) 266-4301

Activity Location: *Hudson Valley, N.Y.*

Comments: You can play in many ways at Omega but there is one workshop specifically devoted to play. It includes 50 new games, star wars dodgeball, learning to hang spoons from your nose, balloons, cooperative problem-solving games, and a 6-foot earthball. You'll learn to have fun with a group without special equipment, clothes or money. It's pure play!
Date: Summer

BOARD GAMES

❑ Avalon Hill Game Playing Convention

4517 Harford Road
Baltimore, MD 21214
(301) 254-9200

Comments: Play Avalon Hill games all weekend every August. Other events scheduled during the year where you can meet other avid gamers!

Date: Annual in August   **Time**: All weekend

❑ Exton SCRABBLE Club

Comfort Inn
Exton, PA
(215) 269-1723

Comments: All levels of players here. Beginners welcome but the focus here is on playing tournament SCRABBLE. People come for miles to play here—and socialize too! Associated with the National SCRABBLE Association. Another club in Warminster, PA.

Date: Mondays   **Time**: 8pm

Cost: $5

Contact: Phyllis Patukas

❑ Upper Merion GO Club

317 Huffman Drive, Exton, PA 19341
(610) 363-0574

Activity Location: *Upper Merion Township Building, 175 W. Valley Forge Road, King of Prussia, PA 19406*

Comments: One place this group can be found is Borders where they will teach you the rules of this incredible game and play several games with you. You can join this group and play some serious GO on an ongoing basis! Contact Steve Barberi.

Date: Mondays   **Time:** 7pm

GOLF

❑ Cobbs Creek Golf Course

72nd & Lansdowne Avenue
Philadelphia, PA
(215) 877-8707

Comments: This is a public course with 36 holes and leagues for both men and women. You can find a driving range for practice hitting here too.

❑ Executive Women's Golf League

499 Clover Mill Road
Exton, PA 19341
(215) 363-0966

Activity Location: *Clubs around the area*

Comments: A great opportunity for women who want to play golf and network, this group sponsors a summer tournament. Membership includes clinics, monthly outings, a newsletter, and more. All levels of ability are welcome.
Date: Summers
Cost: $50/Membership and greens fees
Contact: Donna Tenshaw

——— GROUPS FOR RECREATION

❑ American Youth Hostels

35 South 3rd Street
Philadelphia, PA 19106
(215) 925-6004

Activity Location: *Variety of locations*

Comments: Hiking and biking and sailing — and regular outdoor get togethers! AYH sponsors these adult outdoor activities, as well as great travel vacations, including group hiking and biking excursions.
Cost: Reasonable

❑ Dynamic Diversions

> *P.O. Box 42775*
> *Philadelphia, PA 19101*
> *(215) 849-9944*

Comments: These affordable activities range from afternoon walleyball and road rallies to 10-day ski or sail trips. These are really fun, well-run activities with a nice crowd. Newsletter.
Cost: $15/year membership and activity fees
Contact: Joe Feisel

❑ Eastern Cooperative Recreation School

> *80 Valley Road, Apt. C-7*
> *Montclair, NJ 07043*
> *(215) 946-8001 (local contact)*

Activity Location: *Camp Onas in Ottsville, PA*

Comments: This friendly group sponsors weekend and weeklong recreation camps where they participate in games, dancing, singing, drama, and other activities. Events attract a consistent following of all ages as well as newcomers.
Contact: Karen Wisnia

HIKING

❑ Exploratory Walk: Schuylkill River Greenway

> *American Youth Hostels*
> *35 South 3rd Street*
> *Philadelphia, PA 19106*
> *(215) 592-4073 Hotline For Events*

Activity Location: *Royersford Train Station, Main Street, Royersford, PA*

Comments: Exploring for historical trail routes along the river! This and many other neat do-able trips is what you'd do with AYH!

❑ Batona Hiking Club

(215) 659-3921

Comments: Batona takes regular hikes in the Philadelphia area including Pennypack Park, upper trails along the Wissahickon Creek, Conestoga Trail and nearby New Jersey at Lisbon State Forest (Pine Barrens). Watch for weekly hikes in the *Daily News or Inquirer* "Weekend" sections.

❑ Sierra Club Of SE Pennsylvania

623 Catharine Street
Philadelphia, PA 19147
(215) 592-4063

Activity Location: *Academy Of Natural Sciences, 19th & Benjamin Franklin Parkway, Philadelphia, PA*

Comments: Great programs and activities, slide shows, hot environmental topics, action activities, dinners, outings (recently they had a moonlight hike), etc.! Newsletter and a hotline for many upcoming events: 592-4073.

❑ Wanderlust Hiking Club

(215) 580-4847

Activity Location: *Various areas in Philadelphia*

Comments: Sweet hikes of 4-7 miles in nearby areas sponsored by the Philadelphia Department of Recreation. Call for their newsletter which lists upcoming hikes or check under "Nature" in the Friday "Weekend" section of the *Philadelphia Inquirer*.
Date: Saturdays   **Time**: 1:15pm
Contact: Jim Fields

NATURE

❑ Churchville Nature Center

501 Churchville Lane
Churchville , PA
(215) 357-4005

Comments: Indoor and outdoor programs here: travelogs and films, canoeing for experienced canoers, birding, flower walks ("The Edible Garden"), and good socializing!

❑ Friends Of The Wissahickon

Library Company
1314 Locust Street
Philadelphia, PA
(215) 546-3181

Comments: Occasional programs of high quality, for example: Jane Gibson's discussion on "The Industrial History Of The Area." Also weekend lectures outdoors while walking along the Wissahickon, for example, "Exploring An Old Mill." Call for upcoming events.

❑ J. Heinz National Wildlife Refuge At Tinicum

86th & Lindbergh Boulevard
Tinicum, PA
(215) 365-3118

Comments: Nature talks and walks in this superb refuge for all kinds of birds and flowers.

❑ Schuylkill Center for Environmental Education

Hagy's Mill Road
Philadelphia, PA
(215) 482-7300

Comments: This local center presents lectures and workshops concerned with birding, spring migrants, wildlife photography, wild-flower walks, earth journeys, just to name a few!

RACEWALKING CLUB

❑ The Phast Racewalking Club

(302) 998-0720

Activity Location: *Ridley Creek State Park. Also Kelly Drive.*

Comments: This enthusiastic group is out there doing some serious walking. They'll welcome you to join them for short or long walks for racers and non-racers. To racewalk with them regularly, you'll need to join.
Date: Sundays and Tuesdays
Cost: $15/year including classes and newsletter
Contact: Thomas Zdrojewski

RUNNING

❑ Miles For Smiles

Philadelphia Dental Hygienist's Association
523 Somerton Avenue
Philadelphia, PA 19116

Activity Location: *Kelly Drive*

Comments: Just one example of the zillions of charity runs throughout the city. Check under "Sports" in the *Philadelphia Inquirer* "Weekend" section. You can meet other runners before and after running. I did!
Date: October
Cost: $10.00

❑ Broad Street Run

Philadelphia Department Of Recreation
Broad & Sommerville Streets
Philadelphia, PA
(215) 685-0150

Comments: Popular 10-mile charity run sponsored by the City for the American Cancer Society.
Date: 1st Sunday in May
Cost: About $15 entry fee

❑ Great Tulip 10k Run & 12mile Bike Race

Boyertown Area YMCA
301 W. Spring Street
Boyertown, PA 19512
(215) 369-1011

Comments: This is part of the YMCA annual fitness festival. All the Philadelphia "Y's" sponsor exciting runs, walks, and fun runs all over the city in all seasons — something for everybody!
Date: Fall
Cost: Around $10

TENNIS

❑ Tennis Camps Limited

444 East 82nd Street, Suite 31d
New York, NY 10028
(800) 223-2442

Comments: This group runs local tennis summer camps in Swarthmore, PA, with one program especially for singles. Three- or six-day programs with top notch instruction are organized within skill levels, beginners through advanced groups. You can choose daytime classes only or overnight camping.

❑ Tennis Farm

(800) 7-Tennis

Activity Location: *Center City, Chestnut Hill, Wayne, Exton*

Comments: These sessions are organized in 4-week units, meeting twice a week in the evenings. One session includes teaching (all levels) and the other is a round robin adult league. They have very flexible scheduling.
Cost: $232/teaching; $160/round robin
Contact: Andy

MISCELLANY

❑ Archery

Bucks County Fish & Game Association
Turk Road
Doylestown, PA
(215) 348-4421

Comments: Indoor archery in January, February, and March, and an outdoor range for use in warmer months. Seminars and classes offered.
Cost: 1st year: $66; after that: $42/men; $18/women per year

❑ Archery

Middletown Archery
127 Barren Road
Media, PA
(215) 566-8092

Comments: This archery club has a 12-lane indoor range and offers instruction for target shooting and hunting.
Cost: $15 year

❑ Billiards

River City Billiards
4258 Main Street
Philadelphia, PA (Manayunk)
(215) 482-7410

Comments: Nifty little place in the heart of Manayunk. No smoking or drinking, nice ambiance, and comfortable for women to go alone. Lessons on Tuesday and Thursday evenings.
Date: 7 days
Cost: $12/3 classes

❏ Billiards

South Philly Billiards
Whitman Plaza Shopping Center
Front Street & Oregon Avenue
Philadelphia, PA
(215) 339-1970

Comments: Largest billiards hall in the city, they tell us, with 35 pool tables, 1 billiards table and even a mini-pool table. Restaurant, too.

❏ Bowling

Erie Lanes
"M" Street & Erie Avenue
Philadelphia, PA
(215) 535-3500

Comments: This huge bowling hall sponsors many group bowling activities such as league bowling, lessons, special evenings and tournaments.

❏ Fencing

Fencing Academy of Philadelphia
3617-25 Lancaster Avenue
Philadelphia, PA (University City)
(215) 382-0293

Comments: How exciting! Lessons for people ages 7-70, beginners to advanced.
Cost: About $130 for 10 weeks

❏ Frisbee

Philadelphia Area Disc Alliance
(215) 238-8751 (Hotline)

Activity Location: *Various places around the City*

Comments: Tournaments and championship games of Ultimate Frisbee sponsored by these folks. These are "serious" frisbee activities, played all over the city, but they have social events as well. In August there is the Ultimate Frisbee Tournament on Belmont Plateau in Fairmount Park. Call (215) 657-6071 for more information.

GAMES, SPORTS & OUTDOORS

❑ Horseback Riding

Northwestern Equestrian Facility
Northwestern & Germantown Avenues
Philadelphia, PA 19188 (Chestnut Hill)
(215) 685-9286

Comments: Ride outdoors in summer and indoors during fall and winter. Lessons offered. Also a small adult program teaching a few classes like landscape painting.
Cost: Summer $65/4 week & fall $150/10 weeks

❑ Horseback Riding Club

Philadelphia Saddle Club
20 Rose Lane
Flourtown, PA
(215) 233-0341

Activity Location: *Kitchen's Lane in Fairmount Park, Philadelphia, PA*

Comments: A small club for experienced riders who wish accessibility to fine riding horses.
Cost: $250 Membership, then $125/month
Contact: Tom Fitzpatrick

❑ Horseshoe Tournaments

NJ State Horseshoe Pitchers Association
(609) 853-4951
Activity Location: *John Gottone Memorial Park, Oak Road, Vineland, NJ*

Comments: There are lots of great horseshoe players out there! Test your mettle in tournaments where members compete against each other.
Date: Twice a month in summer
Cost: 1st year $12; tournament fee $10

❑ Kite Flying

Annual Philadelphia Kite Festival
(215) 685-0000

Activity Location: *Belmont Plateau, Montgomery Drive and Belmont Avenue, Philadelphia, PA*

Comments: What a fun weekend! Any kite you have will compete! Also they have kite making, kite races, kite hospital, music and food! Call for other events/festivals sponsored by the City.
Date: One April weekend   **Time**: 10am-5pm

❑ Rock Climbing

REI
Ridge & Butler Pikes
Conshohocken, PA
(215) 940-0808

Comments: REI does not offer lessons but use of climbing wall (190' wide, 34' long!) and necessary equipment are free! REI also offers adventure talks every two weeks and other terrific opportunities to meet fellow enthusiasts.
Date: Mondays, Tuesdays, Wednesdays, pm   **Time**: 5:30-8:30pm
          Saturdays, am

❑ Rock Climbing

Base Camp
723 Chestnut Street
Philadelphia, PA
(215) 592-7956

Comments: Local climbers test their skill on an indoor wall in Center City. The Allentown branch of Base Camp offers classes.
Cost: Low fee ($5) or free

GAMES, SPORTS & OUTDOORS
Miscellany

❑ Roller Blading

Bladin' Action
Sporting Club at The Bellevue
Broad & Walnut Streets
Philadelphia, PA
(215) 731-0977

Comments: You have a chance to learn this sexy sport in classes for groups and individuals. Then you can take it out to Kelly Drive when you go to watch the regattas, or go skating around the city with the Philadelphia Landskaters. Looks so cool!
Date: Monday/Wednesday/Friday/Saturday
Cost: $10/Class

❑ Roller Blading

Philadelphia Landskaters
Philadelphia Art Museum, Front Steps
Benjamin Franklin Parkway
Philadelphia, PA
(609) 854-7774

Comments: This terrific, fast expanding group guides beginning and advanced bladers (different days) on trips around the city for learning and fun. This is a multi-age group that is very social, adding hockey games, ski trips, and other activities to their agenda!
Date: Sundays mornings/Tuesdays at 7pm

❑ Roller Dance Classes

Motion Studios
7140 Germantown Avenue
Philadelphia, PA (Mt. Airy)
(215) 242-0660

Comments: One of many dance, fitness, artsy classes given by this innovative organization. See Chapter 4 (Dancing) for additional information.
Date: Saturdays and Tuesdays   **Time**: 8:30-9:30pm
Cost: $8

❑ Swimming

Pennsbury Falconettes Masters
fall (215) 949-6762, summer (215) 547-7974

Activity Location: *Pennsbury School District, 705 Hood Boulevard, Fairless Hills, PA*

Comments: Bring out the Esther Williams (Do you know who SHE is?) in you and become a synchronized swimmer! Or you can just sign up for swimming lessons in this beautiful facility during the day.
Cost: Reasonable
Contact: Betty Hess

❑ Swimming

YMCA — Doylestown Branch
2500 Lower State Road
Doylestown, PA
(215) 348-8131

Comments: Synchronized swimming and water ballet classes. You should know basic swimming strokes before you try this.
Contact: Annette Zaboj

❑ Table Tennis

Shepard Recreation Center
57th Street & Haverford Avenue
Philadelphia, PA
(215) 474-0840

Comments: This City-sponsored center provides opportunities to join others for a game of ping pong — oops, I mean table tennis.
Cost: Free

❑ Tae Kwon Do

US Tae Kwon Do Center
4665 Frankford Avenue
Philadelphia, PA
(215) 744-0212

Comments: This beautiful martial art is also taught on Girard Avenue and Bustleton Avenue. The members work out and help teach each other, and have events with other clubs.

❑ Tai Chi

483 Robbins Street
Philadelphia, PA
(215) 725-4569

Comments: Excellent classes taught in a relaxed atmosphere. From beginner to advanced, all Tai Chi forms are taught including Push Hands.
Contact: Jerry Fleischman

❑ Volleyball

YMCA — Roxborough Branch
Ridge Avenue & Domino Lane
Philadelphia, PA (Roxborough)
(215) 482-3900

Comments: This "Y" has a competitive league as well as a non-competitive league for fun only! This and other "Y's" have a million other great activities like Country Dancing and Karate.
Cost: $30/season
Contact: Ro Molyneux

GAMES, SPORTS & OUTDOORS
Miscellany

❑ Walking For Charity

Walkfest
American Diabetes Association
100 N. 17th Street
Philadelphia, PA 19103

Activity Location: *Valley Forge Park & Tyler State Park.*

Comments: Many organizations sponsor runs and walks for good causes like this one. You'll join many cheerful people who like exercising while engaging in charitable activities!
Date: October
Cost: Free with paying sponsors

Health & Fitness

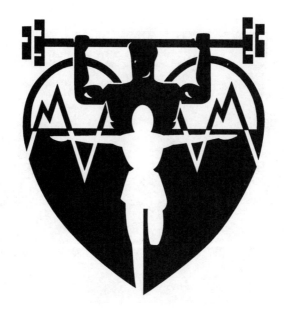

Nutrition
Personal Growth
Walk
Wellness
Yoga & Meditation

A meditation at the Shambhala Center.

HEALTH & FITNESS

Many of the activities in this book will contribute to your good health and physical fitness, such as those listed in GAMES, SPORTS & OUTDOORS. Just reading this book and planning new ways to do interesting and pleasurable things contributes to your good psychological health! However, the specific importance of the activities in this chapter is that the exploration of health issues is their *central* purpose. So if you want to do things that are healthy, look at *all* the activities in the book. If you really want to concentrate on HEALTH & FITNESS issues (embarking on a "healthy journey," as some of us put it), the activities listed in this chapter can get you started.

Actually, there are two overall types of activities in this chapter: Classes that teach better health practices, and personal growth activities which expand your physical, mental and/or spiritual experience. Some of the best classes in the area that are reasonable in cost can be found at local hospitals such as **Hahnemann, Jefferson**, and **Graduate**. They sponsor lectures/discussions by experts and small groups for support. They also have ongoing learning in areas of common concern, such as Stopping Smoking, Weight Reduction and Stress Management. Their ads are quite prominent so you can easily keep up with their programs but if you miss them, call and they will put you on their mailing list. If you're really serious about that health change, you can see that help is available on a regular basis. Once there, you will find other people who share both the wish and the gumption to get off their duff and DO something about it. Are these the types of people you are looking to meet? People who follow through on a wellness plan?

The Personal Growth Activities are more diverse, ranging from academies that offer many courses and certification programs as well as day/weekend workshops for the likes of most of us (**International Academy of Massage Science**), to local individuals offering one specific type of healing approach.

The latter includes one of my personal favorites, **Talia Delone**, whose classes I have attended. Her work integrates movement with insight for healing. Her methods include learning how to create your own dances utilizing the meaning and movement in folk tales in a small group atmosphere of love and creativity. Her workshops were enriching and bonding for those of us participating even though many of us had not known each other beforehand.

There are programs right in your city neighborhood where you can meditate or expand your spiritual understanding. On Sansom Street in Center City there is the Buddhist center, **Shambhala**, a wonderful space to be quiet or take spiritual instruction from local teachers or visiting Buddhist masters. In Manayunk you can find **Yoga on Main** providing Yoga instruction and practice at all levels, and in the South Street area the **Sky Foundation** offers classes and workshops in classical Yoga as well as weekend retreats. Actually, there are many long-standing groups instructing and practicing Yoga in the city. Yoga, which has long been a vehicle for healing and self-awareness for much of humankind, is available in abundance right here in Philadelphia.

There are suburban centers with a wide variety of programs, such as **Creative Energy Options**, where you can find the usual (e.g.,"The Joy of Relaxation") and the unusual (contemplating Emmanuel) for us to peek at, poke around with and consider embracing, in some fashion or another. Some of these workshops or one-shot talks/discussions are reasonable and available to all. Who are the people you meet there? Certainly people whose minds don't run on a narrow track; rather those who truly are open to exploring and exercising their curious interest. And, again, people who *act* on their wish to open their experience and horizons.

Then there are weekend or weeklong retreats far away from Philadelphia, but well attended by Philadelphians. Anyone who has participated in workshops at **Omega**, an adult camp in Rhinebeck, N.Y., speaks with great enthusiasm about their activities. Omega sponsors such a large number of exciting, growthful opportunities that choosing one is very difficult. Workshops include: "Playful Community," "Omega Wellness Program," and "Chinese Culture Retreat." Other retreat communities include **Rowe** in Massachusetts (Bly on "Where Are Men Now;" also, a journal course "Writing For Your Life") and **Kirkridge**, which offers what look to be intensely spiritual and/ or personal experiences in a breathtaking setting in the Berkshire Mountains, *far away* from the stress details of your life.

In a small but specific category, Nutrition, I am totally intrigued by the **Vegetarian Society** which offers many, many evenings of diverse activities related to vegetarian eating. They have talks and discussions, dinners in, dinners out, speakers and trips. The newsletter is fantastic, with great looking recipes, interesting commentary, and interesting upcoming events. Even though I love steak, I've been wanting to visit this energetic group because they are expanding and seem to have so much fun! Another local group offering workshops in alternative health, nutrition and personal growth is in Manayunk, the **Arnold's Way Natural Food Store and Cafe**. I like the neighborhood location, gentle ambiance and would guess that the workshops impart the same atmosphere.

No chapter on HEALTH & FITNESS would be complete without a special mention of the YMCA/YMHA's in the community. They provide high quality, low budget fitness programs for everyone's taste, and are as much part of the community as the library and the local public school. If you are interested in fitness, check them out first. As well, there are many types of 12-step Recovery programs as sources of support, inspiration, and mental health which are located in your very neighborhood — probably even in your local church or synagogue.

Where can you find current listings of these events? The "Life Notes" in the *Philadelphia Inquirer* and the *Daily News* list many of these and more, and the *City Paper* and *Welcomat* "Events" or "Lectures" categories of their weekly activities listings.

All the health and fitness you want is on your doorstep. And the people you meet there want it too.

HEALTH & FITNESS

Fitness Activities • Nutrition

———————————— FITNESS ACTIVITIES

❑ YMCA's & YMHA's

Activity Location: *Many Philadelphia branches*

Comments: Major organizations for group physical activities on a communitywide basis. Local branches city-wide offer aerobics, weight training, tennis and sports, martial arts, swimming, and some real jazzy classes like Modern and Ballroom dance, Volleyball for fun, Walking and Running races, and more! There are also groups for singles only. Be <u>sure</u> to check out your Y!

———————————————— NUTRITION

❑ Essene: The Natural Food Market

719 S. 4th Street
Philadelphia, PA
(215) 922-1146

Comments: This outstanding market and restaurant of healthy food is a kind of hub of natural food activities in Philadelphia. A bulletin board posts notices of natural living activities and healing groups in the area, and interesting "wellness" literature is available.

❑ Pennsylvania Natural Living Conference

350 S. Richland Avenue
York, PA 17404

Activity Location: *Bloomsburg University, Bloomsburg, PA 17815*

Comments: An annual weekend conference in different Pennsylvania locations where people gather to talk about natural methods for staying healthy and healing. Groups discuss subjects like "Diet For A New America," "Food For Life," and "Healing The Impossible."
Date: Annual/August
Contact: Bill Schmidle at (610) 678-4702

❑ Philadelphia Vegetarians

> *Box 41125*
> *Philadelphia, PA 19127*
> *(215) 482-7931*

Comments: An organization that has grown dramatically enjoys regular get-togethers and Sunday dinners out with great conversation, fun, ideas, and support. They will send a detailed newsletter.

PERSONAL GROWTH

❑ Arnold's Way Natural Foods

> *4438 Main Street*
> *Philadelphia, PA 19127 (Manayunk)*
> *(215) 483-2266*

Comments: This place is associated with workshops including: Shiatsu, T'ai-Chi, Yoga, Study Groups in Nutrition, Herbs and Homeopathic Remedies, Bioenergetic Exercises, Empowerment, and Basic Healthy Cooking.

❑ Creative Energy Options

> *Box 603*
> *909 Sumneytown Pike*
> *Springhouse, PA 19477*
> *(215) 643-4420*

Comments: A great variety of programs for wellness including Movement Work, Pain Management, and Loving Touch are presented in on-site classes and weekend retreats. They also hold lectures/ classes for the general public and people in health fields, some featuring well known healers and authors. Call for the calendar.

❑ Heart Of The Goddess

> *10 Leopard Road*
> *Berywn, PA 19312*
> *(215) 644-8276*

Comments: A primary healing center for women in the area. Workshops such as: Woman Wisdom, Women's Drumming Circle, and Motherpeace Tarot are offered.

❑ International Academy Of Massage Science

P.O. Box 277
Glen Riddle, PA 19037
(215) 558-3140

Activity Location: *The Well Person Place*

Comments: This educational organization offers classes, seminars, workshops and study groups in all areas of holistic healing. Examples: Reflexology, Touch For Health, and Therapeutic Touch.

❑ Meditation Workshops For Spring

International House
3701 Chestnut Street
Philadelphia, PA
(215) 292-4540

Comments: Workshops such as: "Power," "Success Is A State Of Mind," "Balance," and "Sensitivity and Survival" were given here in 1993. These were especially designed for people ages 18-28. Check to see if they continue to be available.
Date: April 1993

❑ Kirkridge Retreat & Study Center

Bangor, PA & Lenox, MA
(215) 588-1793

Comments: Holistic workshops such as: "In The Wilderness," "Healing The Wounds," "The Challenge Of Growing Wise," "For The Unemployed," "Life Partners: A Work & Playshop For Couples." This organization employs professional and often well known facilitators.
Cost: About $200/weekend with accommodations.

❏ Omega Institute

260 Lake Drive
Rhinebeck, NY 12572
(800) 862-8890

Comments: A <u>wide</u> range of great workshops in health, professional development, art, social action, or spiritual awareness. Examples: "Music Festival," "Rhythmic Village," "Drums Of Passion," "Playful Community," "Women's Baseball" and more! Call for their terrific catalog. It's huge.
Date: All year but most programs in summer

❏ Rowe Conference Center

Kings Highway Road
Rowe, MA 01367
(413) 339-4954

Comments: Retreat and healing workshops, such as: "Love And Anger," "Poetry And The Imagining Heart," and "Music For Everyone." Professional and accomplished facilitators such as Robert Bly.
Cost: Sliding scale, about $125/weekend

❏ The Life Center

P.O. Box 428
26 Bridge Street
Lambertville, NJ 08530
(609) 397-2541

Comments: A wide variety of healing programs are available in this nearby center, including: "Introduction To Aikido," "Past Lives Seminar," "Study Of Ralph Waldo Emerson Philosophy," and "Sufi Dancing." Several ongoing groups are also available. Call for a calendar of events.

HEALTH & FITNESS

Walk • Wellness

WALK

❑ The Super Cities Walk

National Multiple Sclerosis Society
(215) 963-0100

Activity Location: *Philadelphia Art Museum, Benjamin Franklin Parkway, Philadelphia, PA*

Comments: This walk, one of many walks for charity, also takes place in Delaware, Montgomery, and Bucks Counties. Your physical health improves when you walk for your body and your mental health improves when you walk to help someone else! Watch the papers.
Date: Annual in the Spring

WELLNESS

❑ Graduate Health System

(800) 654-4723

Activity Location: *Various hospital locations in the area*

Comments: Six to eight lectures/discussions by medical professionals per month on current health issues such as: "Headaches and How To Avoid Them," "Arthritis," "Parenting Skills," and "Women and Heart Disease."
Cost: Free

❑ Hahnemann University Community Health

15th & Vine Streets
Philadelphia, PA
(215) 762-8120

Comments: One class offered here, "Dining Out," teaches healthy eating when going to restaurants — with a restaurant trip included! Other great programs, including: "Lifestep" (weight reduction) and "Stress Management," use a small group format for healthy changes.

HEALTH & FITNESS

❑ Thomas Jefferson University Hospital

11th & Walnut Streets
Philadelphia, PA
(215) 955-6319

Comments: Many quality classes to help you get fit, including
Aerobics, Yoga, "Smoke Stoppers," "Weigh To Go," and others!

——————————— YOGA & MEDITATION

❑ Kripalu Yoga Ashram

P.O. Box 250
7 Walters Road
Sumneytown, PA
(215) 234-4568

Comments: This organization teaches Yoga and classes for harmony
between mind and body, and holds retreats in the healing.arts in
Lenox, MA.

❑ Shambhala Center

Wilma Theater (2nd Floor)
2030 Sansom Street
Philadelphia, PA
(215) 568-6070

Comments: An urban Buddhist meditation center which sponsors free
meditation instruction. They also offer group meditations most evenings and Sundays, healing classes, and discussion groups.
Cost: Very reasonable

❑ Sky Foundation

339 Fitzwater Street
Philadelphia, PA
(215) 592-YOGA

Comments: Program for people new to classical Yoga as well as
those who have experience. Weekly classes, workshops, and summer
retreats with visiting teachers and experts in related fields. Non-
denominational.

❑ Yoga On Main

4363 Main Street, 2nd level
Philadelphia, PA (Manayunk)
(215) 482-7877

Comments: Offers a full schedule of Yoga for all levels and ages.

HEALTH & FITNESS

—NOTES —

HOBBIES & CLUBS

BOOKS
BRIDGE CLUBS
CHESS CLUBS
COLLECTING
COMPUTER CLUBS
CRAFTS
FISHING CLUBS

FLEA MARKETS
FOOD & WINE GROUPS
GARDENING CLUBS
HISTORY GROUPS

INTERNATIONAL GROUPS
RADIO CLUB
SCIENCE CLUB
TRAIN CLUB

HOBBIES & CLUBS

Members of the Philadelphia Horticultural Society beautify Philadelphia with new flowers.

HOBBIES & CLUBS

Forward

It is remarkable that once you have discovered an interest in something, you can always find people who share it! I guess it's human nature that we like to associate with others who share our passions, our curiosities, and our areas of interest and knowledge. We like to meet with them, be active with them, tell interest-related jokes, and develop a sense of "my group" with them. In fact, when we don't have such a group, we often feel a bit lonely, like something is missing.

There is a very neat little book called *Organized Obsessions* which lists 1003 clubs around the country. This is a book you want to have around not only because it might help you identify new interests, but also because it is truly fun (and funny!) to see what people get caught up with. A few examples of CLUBS in Pennsylvania are the Marx Brothers Study Unit in New Hope, the Miniature Golf Association in State College, Love Tokens (actual objects) in Huntingdon Valley, the Leif Ericson Society in Media, the James Buchanan Foundation in Lancaster, the International Hug Center in Pittsburgh, and, here in Philadelphia, the Liberty Bell Matchcover group. I list these to let you know how diverse your interests could be, and to encourage you to let your imagination flow into whatever captures your fancy! If it sparks a chord, go for it — and look for fellow enthusiasts!

Let's look at slightly more traditional groups that attract a more general population around Philadelphia. The listing here does not attempt to be exhaustive of all the HOBBIES AND CLUBS in the area. Instead it gives you an overview of the variety of CLUBS around Philadelphia, so you can see what's what. Also it provides kick-off phone numbers for you to begin your search! It was hard not to include tons of my favorite HOBBIES, like gardening — there are lots of gardening clubs like the World Pumpkin Federation or the Daylily Society of America — but I reined in to give you a broad brush of places with interactive events. I do want to mention that many of the

activities listed *throughout* this guide are done by CLUBS that
you can check into.

So what do we have?

CLUBS are great for people who collect things like stamps,
coins, comics, trains, and miscellaneous widgets. The **Chelten
Hills Model Railroad Club** has a sizeable permanent layout for
an HO Model Railroad. They meet weekly to work on it and
share all kinds of information related to the modeling railroad
world. People who love flea markets can find world class
markets in the area such as those in **Englishtown** or
Gilbertsville. If you purchase a "table" and sell regularly, you'll
network with all the folks who are major flea market entrepre-
neurs. If you only sell once, you'll have a day of great chatting
with the sellers around you <u>and</u> the customers perusing your
stuff. If they're interested, you probably have something in
common. Even if you go to buy, you can meet like-minded
people who share your interest in antique chairs, groovy old
tools, or the colonial wooden spoons that you collect.

People who like games need to find other gamers to play
with. Locally we have the **Henry Avenue Chess Club** (in
Andorra), the **Yorktown Bridge Club**, and I just discovered the
Games Workshop on South Street where people interested in
adventure games like "Dungeons & Dragons" can link up with
others in a local games league. People who are joined at the hip
with their computers (like me) love being in the company of
other computer users who know the language, understand the
programs and the problems. **MACBUS** is first class enjoyment,
attended by stimulating people who impart everything you ever
wanted to know about the MAC with a neat sense of humor to
boot! (This book never would have happened had it not been
for MACBUS.) People who love science stuff look for fellow
enthusiasts who <u>also</u> want to know how to get their FCC license
(**Franklin Institute Amateur Radio Club**), or who also are
interested in identifying the star you're looking at

HOBBIES & CLUBS

Forward

(Delaware Valley Amateur Astronomy Society).

Most of the sports clubs are listed in the GAMES Chapter, but one seems more like a HOBBY to me: The **Main Line Fly-Tyers Club**. With great vitality, Dick Baker described the wonderful activities of this group, including notable speakers (Jimmy Carter) giving presentations in meetings that teach and share information about fly-fishing. Then they take trips to the rivers! He made clear that women are in this group as well as men.

Two other areas seem to attract many followers. We search for our roots in groups that illuminate History and Ethnic Culture, whether specific to our particular group or the larger community with which we identify. Nationality-based groups, like the **Polish-American Cultural Museum** and the **German Society**, ethnic and racial groups like those connected to the **Afro-American Cultural Museum** are active in Philadelphia. On a broader scale, the **Balch Institute** describes the development of ethnic groups in this city and the **University Museum of the University of Pennsylvania** traces the cultures of early man. All these organizations have ways for private citizens to take part in their routine, ongoing activities in addition to the special events celebrating that culture. These are volunteer positions; the people you meet there give their time because they extend themselves to contribute to their community. Some historically-oriented groups offer exciting and high action events, such as the celebration of Queen Victoria's birthday **(Victorian Society)**, reenactment of Revolutionary War battles **(Olde Fort Mifflin Historical Society)**, and the Kwanzaa Festival **(Afro-American Cultural Museum)**.

The other extremely popular types of CLUBS are food and drink groups. (Why are you surprised?) There are several fine wine clubs such as the **International Wine Club** and the **American Institute of Wine and Food**, and some include an elegant dinner **(Philadelphia Wine Festival)** which complements the wine — oops, or is it the other way around? The HOBBY of wine is very cosmopolitan, providing considerable information about soil, sun, production style, history of the region, and type of grape. The happy task of drinking it is enhanced by the intellectual understanding of sorting out the flavors you are tasting and guessing which wine it is! It's kind of a puzzle combined with sensual pleasure, especially in the company of others who are enjoying the same experience.

The healthy food CLUBS (**Vegetarians of Philadelphia**) and local macrobiotic groups which meet regularly often have meals together, sometimes cook together, and share information about nutritional wellness. One terrific food-related group is the **Weavers Way Food Co-op** where people work together to supply members with healthy foods. You might bag nuts and raisins with other members, stock shelves on the main floor, or cut cheese for your neighbors. The discussion in the co-op is always lively and you won't mind going to "the store" ever again!

Please take some time thinking about your HOBBIES. "Hobbies" can sound so boring, like something you invent to while away your time. But they are really organized interests where you indulge your curiosity, actively engage in something, and often join together with others around that activity. They provide a structure for ongoing relationships, where, because you have something in common, you feel as though you belong.

HOBBIES & CLUBS

BOOKS

❑ Midlantic Mystery Book Fair/Convention

(215) 923-0211

Activity Location*: Holiday Inn, 4th & Arch Streets, Philadelphia, PA*

Comments: This weekend event includes many activities for mystery book buffs including panels, discussions, networking, meet the (famous) authors, and book signings.
Date: Annual in November

❑ Jane Austen Society

(610) 687-4714

Activity Location*: Radnor Memorial Library, W. Wayne Avenue & Lancaster Pike, Wayne, PA*

Comments: This group talks about Jane Austen's novels, her life and her times.
Contact: Lorraine Hanaway

❑ Philadelphia Science Fiction Society

(215) 957-4004 (Hotline)

Activity Location*: International House, 3701 Chestnut Street, Philadelphia, PA 19104*

Comments: This group has two meetings a month with speakers, often science fiction authors. There is also a sci-fi book discussion group once a month — just show up and participate! Books to discuss are chosen by consensus. PSFS is having a major science fiction conference in November 1994. Great hotline!
Date: 2nd Friday/month   **Time:** 8pm

HOBBIES & CLUBS

BRIDGE CLUBS

❑ Yorktown Bridge Club

(215) 635-2901

Activity Location: *Benjamin Fox Pavilion, Suite 102, Jenkintown, PA 19046, (215) 576-9488*

Comments: A full service club operating 7 days/3 nights a week, this bridge group has special events like hot dog night on Tuesdays, Sunday brunch before the game, and Swiss teams once a month. Classes are offered for all levels. Although this is usually an older crowd, all ages play bridge here.
Contact: Ellen Silverman

CHESS CLUBS

❑ Henry Avenue Chess Group

7901 Henry Avenue
Philadelphia, PA
(215) 487-7751

Comments: All players from beginners to advanced are welcome, including people of all ages. You can find partners here, but it's suggested that you bring a chess set.
Date: Wednesdays   **Time:** 7pm
Contact: Al Hooper

❑ Philadelphia Chess Club

Franklin Mercantile
Near 16th & Walnut Streets
Philadelphia, PA

Comments: No way to call about this — you just have to go and look for these players! You will find partners there for playing and tutors for $7/hour. There is also chess playing in JFK Plaza in the summer.

COLLECTING

❏ Roxborough Coin Club

Roxborough-Manayunk Federal Savings
Ridge & Lyceum Avenue
Philadelphia, PA 19128

Comments: Coin clubs are listed in Sunday's *Philadelphia Inquirer* "View" section. They give no phone numbers so you have to take your chances going there to see what's what.
Date: Wednesdays   **Time:** 7:30pm

❏ Ambler Stamp Club

Trinity Episcopal Church
Bethlehem Pike & Highland Avenue
Ambler, PA

Comments: Stamp collectors looking for fellow stickers can go here or to the Union Methodist church, Allston Road and Brookline, in Haverford. Stamp clubs are also listed weekly in the Sunday *Philadelphia Inquirer* "View" section.
Date: Wednesdays   **Time:** 7:30pm

COMPUTER CLUBS

❏ MACBUS

P.O. Box 403
Huntingdon Valley, PA 19006
(215) 464-6600

Activity Location: *Rohm & Haas Building, 6th & Market Streets, Philadelphia, PA*

Comments: This great computer group is for Macintosh users. They answer all the questions you could possibly raise, have presenters on the latest software (and raffles!), and small interest groups for Desktop Publishing and Small Business Computing. A delightful group and very social with men and women about 75 strong each meeting.
Date: Last Wednesday/month   **Time:** 6:30pm
Cost: $35/year

❑ Philadelphia Area Computer Society

La Salle University
20th Street & Olney Avenue
Philadelphia, PA
(215) 951-1255

Comments: This PC organization meets regularly and sponsors a computer festival in March. There are about 100 computer groups in the area, some focused on specific software packages. You can find them listed in the *Delaware Valley Computer User,* a local paper.
Contact: Steven Longo

CRAFTS

❑ Philadelphia Guild Of Hand Weavers

3705 Main Street
Philadelphia, PA 19128 (Manayunk)
(215) 487-9690

Comments: This active organization, about 300 strong, is interested in all fiber arts such as spinning, felting, handweaving, tatting, caning, etc. They provide classes, workshops, a monthly newsletter and meetings.
Cost: $20/year + workshop fees
Contact: Diane Robertson-Steele

FISHING CLUBS

❑ Fly-Tying Class

Main Line Fly Tyers, Inc.
654 Easton Road
Glenside, PA
(215) 885-0917

Activity Location: *St. Peter's Episcopal Church*

Comments: This sportsmen's (and women's!) group is devoted to fly-fishing and conservation. Each meeting has a demonstration, guest speaker, raffles and chatting about how-to, where to go, etc. They also teach you how!
Cost: $26/year membership
Contact: Dave Baker

HOBBIES & CLUBS

FLEA MARKETS

❏ Englishtown Auction Sales

Old Bridge Road
Englishtown, NJ
(908) 446-9644

Comments: This place is <u>huge</u> — miles and miles of great, campy stuff to sell and lots of chatting between sellers, and sellers and customers. You can rent a table and get rid of all that great stuff in your basement while you're meeting people!
Date: Saturdays and Sundays

FOOD & WINE GROUPS

❏ Wine Festival In The Poconos

American Institute Of Wine & Food
(215) 635-4463

Comments: Among other activities, this group takes excursions to special wine events like the one noted above.

❏ Crab Races Or Clam Shucking Face-Off

Book And The Cook
(215) 636-1666

Activity Location*: Coastal Cave Trading Company, Reading Terminal, 12th & Market Streets, Philadelphia, PA, (215) 627-0568*

Comments: This sounds informative and like good fun. Many BOOK AND COOK events are talks, tastings and signings by famous cookbook authors, often in conjunction with a fabulous meal! Other interesting events include a fish-filleting contest, or preparing excellent sauces. Call for schedule.
Date: Annual in March

❑ Home Sweet Homebrew

> *2008 Sansom Street*
> *Philadelphia, PA 19103*
> *(215) 569-9469*

Comments: Open most afternoons but stop in on this friendly group for free samples on Wednesday nights. Meet beer making compadres and participate in workshops together. Must be 21 years or over.
Date: Wednesdays   **Time:** 12-6pm

❑ International Wine Club

> *Jack's Firehouse*
> *2130 Fairmount Avenue*
> *Philadelphia, PA*
> *(215) 649-9936*

Comments: This group has wine events such as blind tastings many nights of the week. There are also regular presentations at the Friday meetings, including lecture and tasting classes, like "A Tour Of The Rhone." Newsletter and Hotline detailing dates and times of events.
Date: Every other Friday   **Time:** 7pm
Cost: $25

❑ Philadelphia Wine Festival

> *Ritz Carlton Hotel & Philadelphia Magazine*
> *Ritz Carlton Hotel*
> *Philadelphia, PA*
> *(215) 563-1600*

Comments: Elegant dining with others while learning about the corresponding fine wines.
Date: January-April annually
Cost: $45-$95

❑ Vegetarians Of Philadelphia

P.O. Box 24353
Philadelphia, PA 19120
(215) 276-3198

Comments: This is a very active group with picnics, dinners, cooking demos, singing and dancing — these people include great socializing with their veggies! Terrific newsletter of upcoming events and menus.
Contact: Andy

❑ Weavers Way Food Co-op

559 Carpenter Lane
Philadelphia, PA 19119
(215) 843-6945

Comments: This co-op is a center for healthy and fun activities. They bring healthy food to the community for reduced prices but you have to contribute work! You cut cheese, bag nuts, stock shelves with the very interesting people of Weavers Way. Shopping becomes a social experience, but they sponsor social events as well!

GARDENING CLUBS

❑ Hardy Plant Society, Mid-Atlantic

440 Louella Avenue
Wayne, PA 19087

Comments: Write Ms. Mackey to find out how to join. Members attend society meetings, give plant sales, share plants, tour private gardens, and receive a quarterly newsletter.
Cost: $12/year
Contact: Betty Mackey

❑ Getting Down & Dirty: Urban Gardening

Penn State Winter Workshops
Provident Mutual Insurance Building
46th & Market Streets
Philadelphia, PA
(215) 560-4167

Comments: One example of many great Penn State programs. Call for newsletter for events and other courses.
Cost: Free

❑ Pennsylvania Horticultural Society

325 Walnut Street
Philadelphia, PA
(215) 625-8250

Comments: The oldest horticultural society in the U.S. gives workshops/lectures, and sponsor the "Best Garden Contest" every year. They also take bus trips to lovely gardens in the area. Call the hotline for events: 922-8043.
Date: Monday-Friday   **Time:** 9am-5pm
Cost: Free

❑ Greenhouse Gang

Pennypack Watershed Association
2955 Edge Hill Road
Huntingdon Valley, PA
(215) 657-0830

Comments: A neat way to do community service, this group plans and cares for neighborhood landscapes around Pennypack Park.
Date: Tuesdays and Thursdays   **Time:** 10am-12pm

HISTORY GROUPS

❏ Philadelphia Open House

(215) 928-1188

Comments: Tour Philadelphia's elegant townhouses, mansions, country estates, "trinity" houses, artists' lofts and penthouses. Outdoors too, visit Japanese and Victorian Gardens, wildflower and formal gardens. You'll experience 300 years of history, private collections of art and antiques with trained guides, and may include lunch or tea!
Date: Annual in April and May

❏ Afro-American Historic/Cultural Museum

N.W. Corner of 7th & Arch Streets
Philadelphia, PA
(215) 574-0380

Comments: Outstanding events, readings and lectures demonstrating the richness of African-American Heritage. The African-American Genealogy group has open parties. Annual Kwanzaa Festival.
Date: Tuesdays, Saturdays, Sundays **Time:** 10am-5pm
Cost: Adults $4, children and seniors $2

❏ Olde Fort Mifflin Historical Society

(215) 492-1881

Activity Location: *Various historical battlegrounds*

Comments: This group reenacts famous Revolutionary and Civil War battles in full military regalia all over the East coast, but Fort Mifflin is home base. Besides this, people of all ages enjoy two meetings a year and a variety of social events.
Contact: Dori

HOBBIES & CLUBS

❑ University Museum of the University of Pennsylvania

33rd & Spruce Streets
Philadelphia, PA
(215) 898-4000

Comments: Excellent presentations of the world of ancient peoples and traditional cultures. Examples include Egyptian mummies and wooden carvings from Polynesia. They also feature films, concerts, lectures, courses and special events.
Date: Tuesdays and Saturdays & Sundays
Cost: About $2 donation

❑ Victorian Society In America

2026 Kater Street
Philadelphia, PA 19146
(215) 563-9275

Comments: A group interested in the Victorian era, they do historic preservation activities, hear speakers, and have wonderful social events related to the 19th century, such as celebrating Queen Victoria's birthday and a Spring Pub Crawl!
Cost: $15/year plus expenses for each event
Contact: Leslie Lynch Clinton

INTERNATIONAL GROUPS

❑ Balch Institute

18 S. 7th Street
Philadelphia, PA
(215) 925-8090

Comments: Explore your family history! Balch displays photos, artifacts and descriptions of early community life in Philadelphia They sponsor discussions about ethnic culture and immigration history as well as a dinner club and field trips for singles and couples!
Date: Monday-Saturday   **Time:** 10am-5pm
Cost: Donation

❑ German Society Of Philadelphia

611 Spring Garden Street
Philadelphia, PA
(215) 627-2332

Comments: Presentations about notable German people and culture with dinners and other social events. New people are welcome to take part in these activities!

❑ Polish American Cultural Museum

308 Walnut Street
Philadelphia, PA
(215) 922-1700

Comments: You can join the Museum and enjoy displays on Polish history, lectures, dinners together, excursions and newsletter. You can also volunteer and be a part of the hosting.
Date: Monday-Saturday   **Time:** 10am-4pm
Cost: Free

RADIO CLUB

❑ Franklin Institute Amateur Radio Club

Franklin Institute
20th Street & the BF Parkway
Philadelphia, PA
(215) 448-1139

Comments: This amateur ham radio club which is open to the public shares radio related information and can help you obtain your FCC license. You can also call the American Radio Relay League (203) 666-1541 for a list of amateur radio clubs near you.
Date: 1st Wednesday/month   **Time:** 7:30pm
Contact: Henry Disston

HOBBIES & CLUBS

SCIENCE CLUB

❏ Delaware Valley Amateur Astronomy Society

(215) 836-9266

Activity Location: *Schuylkill Center for Environmental Education, Philadelphia, PA (Roxborough)*

Comments: This group has good sized meetings (about 70) with speakers and discussions. Occasional public star gazing parties. Newsletter. Also a center city group: The Rittenhouse Astronomical Society which often meets at the Franklin Institute.
Date: 2nd Friday/month
Contact: Al Lamperti

MISCELLANY

❏ Chelten Hills Model Railroad Club

Reading Train Station (Retired)
8000 Old York Road
Elkins Park, PA
(215) 357-3990

Comments: This group has a 25' x 52' layout for the HO Modeling Railroad which they upgrade on a weekly basis. There is an annual open house and demonstration on three winter weekends. All ages of men and women are invited to try this activity.
Date: Thursdays   **Time:** 7:30pm-11pm
Contact: John Walz

❏ Walt Disney Club

National Fantasy Fan Club
P.O. Box 281
Broomall, PA 19008
(215) 353-3698

Comments: A club for Disneyana enthusiasts, who receive newly released merchandise, events info, a newsletter, and raffles!
Date: 1st Sunday/month   **Time**: 1pm
Contact: George Hattersley   **Cost**: $15/year

Music

CHORAL SINGING

CLASSES

CLASSICAL - LISTENING & DISCUSSING

CLASSICAL - ORGANIZATION

CLASSICAL - PERFORMING

DRUMMING/GUITAR/BASS

FOLK

IRISH

JAZZ

LATIN

OPERA

SONGWRITING

Fiddle jam at the Philadelphia Folk Festival.

Most of us love MUSIC. We play our CD's or the radio all the time. It influences our moods, pushes us to dance, move swingy, sing in our showers, and sets the stage for our activity alone and with others. But many of us don't know how to be active with MUSIC. We don't *do* MUSIC if you know what I mean. For those of you who wish you were actively mixing it up in some way with the MUSIC you love, this chapter is for you.

There is so much terrific MUSIC being made in Philadelphia. You probably know some wonderful places to be musical that are not in this book. (Please tell me so I can add it to the next edition!) What I have included is a smattering of interactive music goings-on that give you an entree into a variety of musical experiences, depending on your interests. They are all reasonable in cost and involve friendly, interested people. By the way, both the *Welcomat* and the *City Paper* have outstanding listings for MUSIC events for every day of the year. Another way to learn more about the MUSIC events that interest you is to go to one event of that type. The people there will know of others and the information will snowball in your direction.

The *sampling* of musical activity events listed here are events in which interaction with people is built in, a requirement that seems to favor certain types of activity. The list includes things that I have done myself and love, so there will be an unintentional selection factor here.

SINGING. Ah, singing! Like dancing and art, singing is something you do because you are human — it is your birthright. You do *not* sing because you have a beautiful voice or can "carry a tune." Those are performance standards some unhappy person thought up to keep us from having joyful fun. You sing because you want to make music or just because you feel good! Now there are places to sing where you have to have a beautiful voice and carry a tune, such as **Singing City** or the

Mendolssohn Club. They make cash money to perform, so their singers have to make music other people recognize and truly enjoy listening to. To sing with them you need to audition and sound very, very pretty. However they are not professionals; they are semi-pros, and <u>you</u> might be that good. If you think you might be, you can try out and see. No harm in that. (My voice is mediocre but I was let into a terrific Renaissance Group because they needed an alto and I didn't hurt them any. What an outstanding experience that was for me! So you never know.) And if you can't be a regular member of the group, for about $12 you can sing the "Messiah" (and other works) with Singing City for an afternoon in March. I mean — <u>you</u> stand in the middle of the Singing City Singers and add your voice to this amazing sound — it's incredible! The Singers are very gracious and it is a very special afternoon. Another way to sing choral music is to join a chorus like the **Temple Center City Chorus** with about 35 other happy, ordinary singers and sing a nice range of music culminating in a performance. There are also choruses in a number of adult education programs or high school extension classes.

Other major singing opportunities are sponsored by various folk song groups, most notably, the **Philadelphia Folk Song Society**. This group puts on various events during the course of the year, the most famous being the **Philadelphia Folk Festival** held in Schwenksville in late August. This remarkable yearly gathering of both national and local performers on-stage and many, many folk music lovers from everywhere, watching, singing, and dancing off-stage, is a superb event. The weekend is so filled with music that words can't get around it — you have to be there. (By the way, if you can stand the dirt, maybe mud, camping is the way to go; the-middle-of-the night bonfire music is fabulous!) PFSS also holds two mini-folk festivals in fall and spring in the Philadelphia suburbs with dancing workshops, singing and performing. For a regular diet of folk singing, the Folk Song Society gets together to sing in members'

homes once a month. Other places to sing include two Open Circles, one at the **Mermaid Inn**, the other at the **Folk Factory** in Mt. Airy, where there are all kinds of performing and open audience singing.

PLAYING. Moving on to instruments (You thought I'd never get off SINGING, didn't you?), one organization that offers a wide range of very inexpensive classes for instrumental music is **Settlement Music School**. So does **Temple Center City** where you can take classical training on many instruments or learn guitar and jazz playing, such as drumming and percussion. Some instruments are hard to learn and some are easy, like the recorder, but all make fabulous music, and can be enjoyed in ensemble playing. For example, for jazz improvisation you can get involved with the **ClefClub** in West Philadelphia where all musicians are welcome to bring their instruments. As for classical playing, there are community orchestras all over Philadelphia, such as the **Chestnut Hill Community Orchestra** and orchestras of small organizations such as the **Orchestra at Immaculata College** which frequently looks for members. There is a great community of non-professional musicians in Philadelphia forming small quartets and trios playing for pleasure. What would it take to be among them?

Activity in musical areas gets pretty sophisticated and demonstrates a real commitment when you go away to camp to do it. Summer workshops at **Augusta Arts Center** in West Virginia are week-long and teach beginners and advanced students the specialty areas of dance and music-making like Bluegrass, banjo and vocalizing, to name a few. It is high quality learning and doing, reasonably priced and enormous fun. In New York state, **Omega** provides a raft of music experiences, some related to healing and self-discovery, lasting a week or a weekend, also low in cost. Lots of Philadelphians go to Omega and Augusta and come back with a network of

music-making friends. You don't have to be a kid to get to go to summer camp and come back refreshed and transformed!

ENJOYING/LISTENING. There are ways for you non-performers to be really active with music and meet others who share your musical interests. Some performances are followed by lectures, discussions and meeting-composer opportunities. For example, the **Philadelphia Orchestra** holds Post Concert Conversations with members of the performing group. The **University Museum** has "Concerts & Croissants" on Sunday mornings, a concert followed by an informal brunch in a lovely setting. And of course you can join groups such as the **Chamber Music Society** allowing you to be supportive of the group and join others actively involved in promoting the fine cultural arts we have in Philadelphia.

Many of the folk music concerts, such as those held at the **Cherry Tree**, are very casual and interactive, providing natural opportunities to talk to other attendees. Likewise, jazz events like Saturday noon at the **Reading Terminal**, or **Ortliebs**, or **Jazz Vespers**, are attended by friendly people including those who enjoy connecting through their love of music.

I'm happy to say there is revived interest in opera in Philadelphia which means there is some terrific listening here. Several clubs which provide members opportunities to join together to listen to and discuss opera include the **Opera Club** which meets in Center City and the **JMS Branch Settlement School** in Jenkintown which puts together some fabulous Opera Trips. They both have newsletters to help you plan your music group schedule.

Whether you are singing and dancing together, playing an instrument with a small group, taking a class or engaging in a discussion, Philadelphia is an excellent place to find others who love to do the same and want to do it with you.

CHORAL SINGING

❑ Mendelssohn Club
(215) 735-9922

Activity Location*: Academy of Music & Churches in the area*

Comments: For those of you who can really sing, here's your chance! This group holds auditions which are open to the public for semi-professional singers. The same is true for the Choral Arts Society (545-8634) and Singing City (561-3930). It doesn't hurt to try!

❑ Sing In!
Singing City Choir
2031 Chestnut Street
Philadelphia, PA
(215) 561-3930

Activity Location: *Various Center City Churches*

Comments: If you can't be a "regular" member of a great chorus, you can join the fabulous Singing City Choir for an afternoon of singing choral masterpieces. They hold several Sing-Ins a year and do the Messiah one time. It is thrilling! (Look for me!)
Date: Sundays   **Time:** Afternoons
Cost: About $10 for Sing In!

❑ Center City Chorus
Temple University Center City
1616 Walnut Street
Philadelphia, PA
(215) 204-4353

Comments: You need only to be able to carry a tune to make beautiful music with this congenial group that sings a varied repertoire of choral music — including folk and popular songs.
Cost: About $60 for 12 Wednesdays

CLASSES

❑ Settlement Music School

416 Queen Street
Philadelphia, PA
(215) 336-0400

Comments: Settlement provides some of the finest classes in orchestral/band instruments in the area. They also sponsor concerts by Settlement students that are open to everyone.

❑ Temple University Center City

1616 Walnut Street
Philadelphia, PA
(215) 204-4353

Comments: In Fall 1993, the adult music education classes included lessons in voice and instruments, and "Jazz Ensemble/Improvisation," "Enjoying Classical Music and Opera," "Becoming a Perceptive Listener," and more. Check their excellent catalog!

❑ Temple University Music Prep

Temple University Center City
1616 Walnut Street
Philadelphia, PA 19103
(215) 204-1512

Comments: Experienced musicians, rank beginners, or serious listeners will all find many learning opportunities here. A wide diversity of classes are offered to help you learn how to read a score, play an instrument, enhance your listening, learn about Mozart, and sing in a chorus.

❑ University Of Pennsylvania: College Of General Studies

3440 Market Street, Suite 100
Philadelphia, PA
(215) 898-1147

Comments: In Fall 1993 Penn's adult education classes included: "Intro to the History of Music," "Music Theory for Non-Music Majors," "Jazz: Style and History, Haydn and Mozart" and more! A great place to begin deepening your music appreciation.
Date: Fall 1993

CLASSICAL - LISTENING & DISCUSSING

❑ Pennsylvania Pro Musica

225-A S. 42nd Street
Philadelphia, PA
(215) 222-4517

Activity Location: *Church Of Holy Trinity, Rittenhouse Square, Philadelphia, PA*

Comments: This sophisticated musical group plays a variety of interesting ensemble music with refreshments and has a devoted following.
Cost: $8-18

❑ Post Concert Conversations

Philadelphia Orchestra
Academy Of Music Ballroom
1420 Locust Street
Philadelphia, PA 19102
(215) 893-1900

Comments: After some concerts you have a chance to talk to soloists, conductor and/or composer. To find out which concerts and about other orchestra activities, call for the concert guide.
Cost: Free with ticket from concert.

❑ Concerts & Croissants

University Museum String Orchestra
University Museum Cafe
33rd & Spruce Streets
Philadelphia, PA 19104
(215) 898-4015

Comments: Music followed by a reception in a cozy situation. The same group also holds free concerts on winter Sundays at 2:30pm.
Date: Sundays   **Time:** 11:30am

CLASSICAL - ORGANIZATION

❑ Classical Music Lovers' Exchange

Box 31
Pelham, NY 10803

Comments: Nationwide link between unattached music lovers.

❑ Friends Of Philadelphia Chamber Music Society

Philadelphia Chamber Music Society
135 S. 18th Street
Philadelphia, PA 19103
(215) 569-8587

Comments: Join the Chamber Music Society to be involved with this premier Philadelphia arts organization.

CLASSICAL - PERFORMING

❑ Immaculata College & Community Orchestra

(215) 647-4400 Ext. 3473
Immaculata, PA

Comments: This college community orchestra seeks new members for all sections of the orchestra.
Date: Thursdays   **Time:** 7pm-9:30pm
Contact: Sister Regina Foy

❑ Philadelphia Classical Guitar Society

2038 Sansom Street
Philadelphia PA
(215) 567-2972

Comments: Guitar concerts, workshops, discussions, and lectures
Contact: David Temple at (215) 925-6866

CONFERENCE

❑ Augusta Heritage Arts Workshops

Augusta Heritage Center
Davis & Elkins College
Elkins, West Virginia 26241
(304) 636-1903

Comments: Five weeks of traditional music, crafts, dance and folklore. Classes include: banjo, Bluegrass, Blues, folk painting, leatherworking, stepdance, vocal week, weaving, storytelling, and more great music!
Date: Summer
Cost: Classes start at $155/week

❑ Music And Healing Institute

Immaculata College, Depart ment of Music
Immaculata, PA 19345
(215) 647-4400 Ext. 41

Comments: The purpose of this Institute is to nurture one's vision and meaning of one's "inner music" in order to promote holistic and spiritual well being. Immaculata offers weekend and evening programs of this type as well.
Date: Annual in August

❏ Omega Institute

260 Lake Drive
Rhinebeck, NY 12572
(800) 862-8890

Comments: Many unique and exciting music programs: "Songwriting for Women," "Singing for Brave People," " Music-Making for Everyone," "Ensemble Singing," and "Building a Vocal Community" are some examples of what you will find here.
Date: Mostly in summer

DRUMMING/ GUITAR/BASS

❏ Sam Ash Music Stores

2100 Rte. 38
Cherry Hill, NJ
(609) 667-6696

Comments: Seminars and workshops led by notable musicians on a periodic basis. Call to be on mailing list for events.

❏ Pro Drum Center

363 North Easton Road
Glenside, PA
(215) 887-1462

Comments: Hand drumming on Monday, Tuesday, Thursday, Friday and Open Drum Circle Jam session every Friday. Workshops for beginner and advanced drummers. All types of percussion instruments are welcome in jamming.

FOLK

❑ Open Circle

Mermaid Inn
Mermaid Lane & Germantown Avenue
Philadelphia, PA (Chestnut Hill)
(215) 247-9797

Comments: A wonderful group of people who sing, play, and recite poems — and you can perform with them or just listen and enjoy! Also, many other neat events take place at the Mermaid, including dancing and music making of all kinds.
Date: 1st & 3rd Thursdays.   **Time:** 8:30pm

❑ Second Sunday

Miryam's Farm
6815 Tohickon Hill Road
Pipersville, PA
(215) 766-8037

Comments: Music to hear, craft demonstrations (examples: "Understanding Crystals," "Stenciling") and fellowship are presented in this comfortable and pastoral setting.
Date: 2nd Sunday/month   **Time:** 2pm
Cost: Donation

❑ Folk Factory Coffee House

Unitarian Universalist Church
Stenton Avenue at Gorgas Lane
Philadelphia, PA (Mt. Airy)
(215) 848-6246

Comments: Good place to enjoy performers, open mike, and open circle (everyone can sing along). Quiet games are available while you listen.
Date: 2nd Friday/month   **Time:** 8pm
          4th Thursday/month

❏ "Sekere" Workshop

Folklife Center
International House
3701 Chestnut Street
Philadelphia, PA 19104
(215) 387-5125, Ext . 2219

Comments: A workshop where you make an African percussion instrument and learn to play it! This example features Philadelphia's Women's Sekere Ensemble and includes materials.
Cost: $45

❏ International Music Series

International House
3701 Chestnut Street
Philadelphia, PA
(215) 895-6537

Comments: A great diversity of musical performances happen here. International house also has great film, dance and lecture/discussion programs. Call to receive the *In House Newsletter* which lists upcoming events.

❏ Spring Thing

Philadelphia Folk Song Society
7113 Emlen Street
Philadelphia, PA
(215) 247-1300

Comments: Miniature version of the August Folk Festival. Folksinging, instruments, storytelling, and dancing with a similar event in October called the Fall Fling.
Date: Memorial Day weekend

❏ Philadelphia Folk Song Society

7113 Emlen Street
Philadelphia, PA
(215) 247-1300

Comments: If you want to be involved with folk music, <u>this</u> is the group that does folk activities in the area. They sponsor monthly folk singing in PFSS members' homes and occasional workshops. Receive the newsletter of happenings when you join.

❏ The Philadelphia Folk Festival

Philadelphia Folk Song Society
7113 Emlen Street
Philadelphia, PA
(215) 247-1300

Activity Location: *Old Pool Farm, Schwenksville, PA*

Comments: Four full days of fabulous big name folk music, dancing, juggling, crafts and fun. Camping available where great Bluegrass and folk singing goes on all night long around bonfires. Don't miss this great Philadelphia experience! There are two smaller festivals in the fall and spring.
Date: Late August

❏ The Cherry Tree Music Co-Op

St. Mary's Parish Hall
3916 Locust Walk on Penn Campus
West Philadelphia, PA
(215) 386-1640

Comments: Sunday night concerts in Philadelphia's eclectic coffee house. Mini folk festivals and other events take place here too. To be more involved, you can join the volunteer staff.
Date: Sundays

❑ Troubadour Folk Club

Churchville Nature Center
501 Churchville Lane
Churchville, PA 18966
(215) 357-4005

Comments: Come for open singing, concerts and discussions about various musical topics such as "Care Of Instruments." This group also sponsors a great annual Folk Faire with music and activities.
Date: 2nd & 4th Tuesdays/month **Time:** 8pm
    2nd Saturday/month
Cost: $5

IRISH

❑ Philadelphia Ceili Group

Commodore Barry Club
6815 Emlen Street
Philadelphia, PA
(215) 849-8899

Comments: A great place to be for Irish music and Ceili dancing where beginners can learn Ceili dancing on the same night! Terrific top name Irish performers do Irish "jamming."
Date: Friday nights

❑ Irish Music & Dance Festival

Philadelphia Ceili Group
6815 Emlen Street
Philadelphia, PA 19119
(215) 849-8899

Activity Location: *The Cannstatter Club, 9130 Academy Road, Philadelphia, PA*

Comments: A weekend festival of Ceili — with Irish musicians, workshops and beginning and advanced step dancing.
Date: September

JAZZ

❑ Ellen Rose Restaurant

5920 Greene Street
Philadelphia, PA
(215) 843-1252

Comments: Relaxed atmosphere to listen to music, have a nice supper, and chat with people there.
Date: Fridays   **Time:** 9:30pm

❑ Jazz Vespers

Old Pine Street Church
4th & Pine Streets
Philadelphia, PA
(215) 925-8051

Comments: Jazz musicians integrate their music into a spiritual celebration.
Date: 3rd Sunday/month   **Time:** 5pm

❑ Ortlieb's Jazz Haus

847 N. 3rd Street
Philadelphia, PA
(215) 922-1035

Comments: Good jazz club features some of the best jazz people in the area. Parking in supervised lot.
Date: Every night
Cost: No cover!

❑ Sunday Jazz Jam

Philadelphia ClefClub of the Performing Arts
The Cornocopia
4942 Parkside Avenue, 2nd floor
Philadelphia, PA

Comments: Reviving a great tradition of good music and fellowship, all musicians welcome to bring your instruments.
Date: Sundays   **Time:** 7pm

LATIN

Asociacion De Musicos Latino Americanos

P.O. Box 50296
Philadelphia, PA 19132
(215) 634-4150

Comments: A multicultural organization that welcomes people in all walks of life to volunteer, take classes in Latin dance and percussion, and attend performances and workshops. They say their music is hot and the atmosphere is joyous!

OPERA

❑ For The Love Of Opera

Gail Tomas
Westview Street & Carpenter Lane
Philadelphia, PA 19119 (West Mt. Airy)
(215) 849-1616

Comments: Julliard grad and singer Gail Tomas teaches four-week classes in an informal, interactive atmosphere on specific operas or on opera topics.
Date: Every other Wednesday   **Time:** 7pm
Cost: About $50 for 4-5 classes

❑ Delaware Valley Opera Company

Hermitage Mansion
700 E. Hermit Lane
Philadelphia, PA
(215) 424-5980

Comments: Wonderful opera followed by a social hour and a light buffet meal.
Cost: About $15

❏ JMS Branch Settlement School

> *515 Meetinghouse Road*
> *Jenkintown, PA*
> *(215) 885-3345*

Comments: Join hundreds of exuberant opera lovers who enjoy the stimulating and fun trips to matinees at Lincoln Center and other cities.
Contact: Phyllis Silver

❏ Opera Club

> *1346 Joan Drive*
> *Southampton, PA 18966*
> *(215) 322-1364*

Activity Location: *Philadelphia Senior Center, 509 S. Broad Street, Philadelphia, PA*

Comments: Opera lovers discuss opera and related arts, preview local operatic productions, feature singers and conductors at their gatherings, all in a lively informal atmosphere.
Cost: $5/meeting but free to members
Contact: Florence Mclaughlin

SONGWRITING

❏ Philadelphia Songwriters Forum

> *Northeast Regional Library*
> *Cottman Avenue & Oakland Street*
> *Philadelphia, PA*
> *(215) 685-0592*

Comments: A forum for discussion, exchange of ideas and learning for beginner and advanced songwriters. Bring a tape or play your song on piano or guitar. Call to be on mailing list.
Date: Mondays   **Time:** 7pm
Cost: Free

MUSIC

— NOTES —

Non-Alcoholic Socializing

COFFEEHOUSES

DANCE CLUBS

DESSERTS

EXERCISE & FITNESS

OUTDOOR ACTIVITIES

TEA-TIME

VACATIONS

Sober Sailing adventures.

A Saturday night at HP's sober club.

NON-ALCOHOLIC SOCIALIZING
Forward

Let me level with you. This is the chapter that inspired this book. There was a time when I wondered if all impromptu social activity took place in bars and clubs, especially the kind of social activity that involved meeting new people, for both romance and friendships. I knew there was a lot of social activity in people's homes, parties and such. But I wondered about the type of thing where you say: "I'd like to socialize tonight, have fun and meet some new people, where do I go?" Most people think of clubs and bars. But what if you don't want to be around alcohol when you are out socializing? Where do you go?

Here are several suggestions:

1) Be prepared: Develop a diverse network of friends who enjoy certain kinds of non-alcoholic socializing themselves. Where do you find them? Look into renewing contact with old high school/college chums. Get together with current friends and bring together friends of friends to meet each other for a non-alcoholic brunch. Check out your favorite activities in this book and over time get to know some of the other participants. Then ask them to do a movie or coffee. Having about 4-5 people ("regulars") to go places with really helps in going out to meet other new people — maybe to a sober dance, or somewhere you can play billiards, or to explore the new art world on **First Friday**, or the **Saturday night Swing Dance**!

2) Try to have an activity that repeats on a regular basis: the Sunday morning bike ride with the **Philadelphia Bike Club**, a sketching class at **Fleisher**, aerobics at the "**Y**" or an exercise club. Having regular non-drinking social activity keeps you from feeling stale and bored, and reminds you of how good you feel being active and involved. When you are busy doing things you like, you are less inclined to feel restless about checking out the bar scene.

3) <u>Look into some of the following activities</u> (the ones noted are examples of each):

Coffeehouses

Coffeehouses are typically places where people go to talk (**Last Drop Cafe**). They might also read, but generally there is a conversational atmosphere. Topics floating around include politics, books, and music, with an occasional reading or recital to get things started. Some places have games like chess, GO or backgammon on tap and you can surreptitiously look over a player's shoulder or play yourself! The atmosphere is relaxed and mellow and no one is drinking. Watch for these happenings in coffeehouses by looking in *City Paper* and *Welcomat* "Events" sections or just stop by.

Desserts

I *have* met new people for conversation in terrific little dessert places, but it's a bit chancy. Maybe they should have Friendship Tables where people who are alone sit at designated tables with other single diners and enjoy a conversation while sipping or sampling a fine confection. Even without Friendship Tables, these places are often pretty intimate. Lots of people do go alone to charming dessert places and read the paper while they drink their coffee (**Capriccio**) — it's a cool thing to do and sometimes you can begin a chat with a person nearby. It's sort of fun to try. If you are with a friend enjoying a luscious dessert (**Pink Rose**) you might try extending your conversation to include others, if they're reading the latest book by your favorite author (or whatever). Consider it!

Tea Time

All of the above goes for places to drink Tea, except Tea places (**Ritz Carlton**) are usually more formal and starting conversations is harder. It's just that these are fun and different places to go where the *focus* is clearly not on alcohol, even if it is served there. Having Tea is a lovely thing to do, especially if you really get into it (wear a hat, an ascot, your best earrings, a long slender Garbo coat — you know what I mean!).

Activities Earmarked For People Who Are Sober

If you want to socialize with people interested in recovery, there are some wonderful things going on that are especially for recovering people which are identified in this listing as "sober" in the **Comments**. They include social dance clubs (**New Alternatives**), an exercise club with games (**Time Out**), outdoor activities groups (**Adventures in Sobriety**), support groups for Recovery (**Starting Point**), sailing (**Sober Sailing**), and a variety of vacation opportunities (**Serenity Trips**) that include sports like biking, hiking, boating, excursions and tours.

This book originated as an effort to find places to go, have fun and meet people in groups connected by interests. Consequently, throughout this book are activities where the strongest drink is 7-Up. Many are activities where only very occasionally are alcoholic beverages a minor part of what's going on. Most of the action is directed to doing things together and getting things done.

With a bit of scratching around, you'll dig up your own wonderful activities that have been designed for people who want to have a great time with their heads on straight! They **are** out there. The world is "the oyster" for the non-users too!

COFFEEHOUSES

❏ Borders Book Shop & Espresso Bar

1717 Walnut Street
Philadelphia, PA
(215) 568-7400

Comments: One of the first coffee bars housed and integrated with other events. You can enjoy weekly free concerts, book and story readings, game nights and a variety of other unique and active evenings in a sober, smoke-free atmosphere. These places get great reviews from everyone — a very successful mix! Other locations are Bryn Mawr, Marlton, NJ, and Chestnut Hill.
Date: Everyday

❏ Caribou Cafe

1121 Walnut Street
Philadelphia, PA
(215) 625-9535

Comments: Jim Quinn says "As elegantly homey as a Paris bistro." Great place to talk French or talk about anything.
Date: Everyday
Cost: Reasonable

❏ Centerstage

Actors Center in the Bourse Building
21 S. 5th Street
Philadelphia, PA
(215) 925-6400

Comments: This cafe with a drama focus even has a drama bookstore. A theater group which you can join performs here and there is an open mike especially for recovering people on Monday nights.

❑ Folk Factory

> *Unitarian-Universalist Church*
> *Stenton Avenue & Gorgas Lane*
> *Philadelphia, PA*
> *(215) 848-6246*

Comments: Coffee and tea in this warm conversational atmosphere in Mt. Airy where folk music is the entertainment.
Date: 2nd Friday/month   **Time:** 8pm
        4th Thursday/month

❑ IPSO

> *517 S. 5th Street*
> *Philadelphia, PA*
> *(215) 922-6784*

Comments: Go here to talk about Italy, talk about books, or about anything else. Great cappuccino and friendly atmosphere, speakers and poetry readings all happen here. Stop in and pick up their fliers.
Date: Everyday
Cost: Reasonable

❑ Itchy Foot Coffeehouse

> *4620 Griscom Street*
> *Philadelphia, PA*
> *(215) 426-9408*

Comments: Has music on some Saturdays.

❑ Makam's Kitchen

> *24th and Lombard Streets*
> *Philadelphia, PA*
> *(215) 546-8832*

Comments: Coffeehouse with deep conversations and good food. Often a younger crowd.
Date: Closed Mondays

❑ Acoustic Cabaret

> *Old City Coffee*
> *221 Church Street*
> *Philadelphia, PA*
> *(215) 629-9292*

Comments: In an intimate atmosphere, music on some weekend nights. Call to check on music nights or look in the *City Paper*. No smoking.
Cost: $5 Cover

❑ The Last Drop Coffee House

> *13th & Pine Streets*
> *Philadelphia, PA*
> *(215) 893-0434*

Comments: Many students, much discussion all around, comfortable surroundings, poetry readings and music performed. Great place!

DANCE CLUBS

❑ HP's

> *311 N. 3rd Street*
> *Philadelphia, PA*
> *(215) 625-9744*

Comments: You'll find many non-alcoholic activities here. It's a large place for dancing and games like arcades, billiards, and cards. Coffee and food are available so you can sit at tables and chat. Every third month, they sponsor a business card networking activity. An all around social club that really starts "happening" about 11 pm!
Date: Fridays & Saturdays   **Time:** 9pm-3am
Contact: Gary Feldman

NON-ALCOHOLIC SOCIALIZING

Dance Clubs • Desserts

❏ New Alternatives

923 N. Watts Street
Philadelphia, PA (N. Philly)
(215) 763-2966

Comments: This sober club has a large dance floor with slow and fast music accommodating a large socializing group. They also have a game room, cards, with a new lounge soon to be added. Happy partying with no substances!

Date: Fridays/Saturdays   **Time:** 10pm-5am

❏ Sobriety Social Set

Fiesta Inn Ballroom
Rte. 611 (Easton Road)
Willow Grove, PA
(215) 947-4185

Comments: A sober group with dances and fun sociable evenings for people who want to dance where there is no drinking.

Date: Saturdays   **Time:** 9:30pm-1am
Cost: $5
Contact: Lisa

DESSERTS

❏ Capriccios

1701 Locust Street
Philadelphia, PA
(215) 735-9797

Comments: This cafe has luscious desserts and exotic teas and coffees. Nice atmosphere — an excellent place to read your paper and chat with people while you sip your cappuccino.

Date: Daily

NON-ALCOHOLIC SOCIALIZING

Desserts • Exercise and Fitness

❑ Ethel Barrymore Room

Hotel Atop The Bellevue
Broad & Walnut Streets
Philadelphia, PA
(215) 893-1776

Comments: Get in touch with your elegant side in this fancy and beautiful setting. Full tea is served with tea sandwiches, scones, and pastry.
Date: Daily   **Time:** 3-5pm
Cost: $12.50

❑ The Pink Rose

630 S. 4th Street
Philadelphia, PA
(215) 592-0565

Comments: A sweet shop that serves tarts, cookies, coffee, tea, espresso and cappuccino. Charming!
Date: Tuesdays-Sundays

EXERCISE & FITNESS

❑ Time-Out

Central YMCA
1425 Arch Street
Philadelphia, PA 19102
(215) 985-2928

Comments: A physical conditioning program where sober people meet have fun and work out! Aerobics, swimming, volleyball, basketball, racquetball, Yoga and martial arts are all offered here.
Date: Tuesdays, Thursdays, Sundays
Cost: $30/month; $4/session
Contact: Mark Wolgin

NON-ALCOHOLIC SOCIALIZING

Outdoor Activities • Tea-Time

OUTDOORS ACTIVITIES

❏ Adventures In Sobriety

Chalfont (Bucks County)
(215) 997-9270

Comments: Open to all ages, this sober group goes hiking, rock climbing, white-water rafting, caving, sailing, etc. Group size ranges from 8-20 and you can sign up for a day trip or longer excursions.
Cost: $25-$54
Contact: Dave Pastorok, Rehab Therapist

❏ Sober Sailing

(215) 923-6435

Activity Location: *Chesapeake Bay*

Comments: Day and weekend sails with occasional extended cruises planned. Beautiful yacht, licensed captain, sailing instructor, and gourmet chef are promised. Great opportunity for sober sailors!
Contact: Richard Gibson

TEA-TIME

❏ The Ritz-Carlton

Liberty Place
17th & Chestnut Street
Philadelphia, PA
(215) 563-1600

Comments: Elegant setting with piano music, fine service and high tea.
Date: Daily   **Time:** 2:30-5pm
Cost: About $10

VACATIONS

❑ Recovery Adventures

> Box 1377
> Brookline, MA 12146
> (617) 734-8884

Comments: Sober vacations run by a social worker. Short trips on the Northeastern coast, including a schooner trip out of Camden, ME, ski weekends in nearby mountains, and rafting on the Penobscot in Maine.
Contact: Andrew Goldstein

❑ Serenity Trips

> 199 Neponset Avenue
> Dorchester, MA 02122
> (617) 825-8532

Comments: Major sober vacations to such places as beaching in Cancun, Mexico, and skiing in Vermont with non-drinking companions.
Contact: George Waterman

❑ Sober Vacations International

> 2365 Westwood Boulevard, Suite 21
> Los Angeles, CA 90064
> (213) 470-0606

Comments: Stats: 60% of this group's clients are single. 55% are female, 45% are male. Trips include Club Med sober programs, trips to the Dominican Republic and a 7-day cruise out of LA.
Contact: Steve Abrams

❏ Sobriety Adventures

Box 542
Grangeville, Idaho 83530
(208) 983-2414

Comments: Rafting trips for 25 people and one counselor. Meetings are held at campsites along the Snake River or the Salmon River Gorge and guides fix the meals!
Date: 2 days/$350; 3 days/$550 + fees and tax
Contact: Scott Fasken

NON-ALCOHOLIC SOCIALIZING

— NOTES —

SENIORS

Especially for Seniors

COMMUNITY SERVICE

FOLK DANCING

LECTURES

SENIOR CENTERS

MUSIC CLASSES

TRAVEL

WORKING VACATIONS

Elderhostelers on a day hike with Appalachian Mountain Club at Pinkham Notch Visitors Center, NH. Photo by Rob Burbank

SENIORS

This is a pretty skimpy chapter, probably because I am almost a SENIOR and want to do what everybody else does. I don't think SENIORS need to be relegated off to SENIOR activities. But this defensive notion on my part misses the point of an "Especially For..." chapter, which is that sometimes we wise mature people <u>want</u> to be with other wise mature people. We want to be with people who not only remember <u>where they were</u> the day that Kennedy was shot, but who also remember what they <u>thought</u> about it because as adults we already had a political philosophy to frame the event. Sometimes we want to hang out with "our own," no matter what the activity, even though we still like doing things with the community-at-large. Thus, a listing of places for SENIORS to find other SENIORS to enjoy.

The activities ESPECIALLY FOR SENIORS require what many seniors have more of than most people: time. Many of the most wonderful experiences offered ESPECIALLY FOR SENIORS are **travel groups** (often reasonably priced), **community service and volunteer groups**, and, a combination of the two: **working (service) vacations**. The travel group I've been hearing about for years from my well-satisfied parents is **Elderhostel** which surely deserves special mention as a vital SENIORS program. As you will see by reading their action-packed catalog, the activities are fabulous — you can't wait to be 55 to qualify. Just think about studying Alpine ecology while living in a rustic dorm at Colorado State and hiking into the beautiful hills each day for classes. Or studying light opera at a music conservatory in Baltimore! A week of this costs less than $325, including everything! They also have working/service vacations which include collaboration with a service community such as **Habitat for Humanity** so you can "give back," while you expand your geographical and personal horizons. Examples of these programs are teaching English to Jamaican schoolchildren, two weeks in Peru studying the effects of the human

population on dolphins, or studying Howler monkey ecology in the Yucatan Peninsula. The only hitch is that you have to be 60 years old (and more) to go.

Who will you meet as you plant trees in the Bayou? Certainly not self-absorbed "the world owes me a living" folks. No, my understanding is that you find the type of person there who knows that in the second part of your life you want to grow in exciting and challenging ways, and who believes that all it requires is the enthusiasm to do so. (Let me not get carried away on this point again!) Other travel groups help you find travelers to join you on trips you both are interested in, so you don't have to drag unwilling friends, and can meet someone new who shares that interest. (If you don't like them, you don't ever have to see them again!) Don't forget to check Chapter 16 on VACATIONS & ADVENTURES for vacations focused on your interests, some of which have specific programs for SENIORS.

Community service opportunities organized ESPECIALLY FOR SENIORS try to capitalize on seniors' skills, like the **Retired Executive Program** where experienced execs give advice and help to new companies at reasonable cost. **AARP** also has a national volunteer program for retirees to give highly skilled services as well as clerical help to overworked and struggling young breadwinners and their companies. Another service program requiring considerable competence that no one ever "taught" you is the **Foster Grandparents** programs in hospitals. They provide interest and nurturance for young children in special care situations. These babies <u>need</u> that love and touching to "thrive" as much as they need food or air. A vital service <u>for</u> Seniors performed <u>by</u> Seniors is political activity. Two organizations particularly active in this arena are the **AARP** and the **Gray Panthers,** which has a strong Philadelphia chapter. With strength in numbers, they perform watch-dog activities relating to issues important to SENIORS, including health care, social security, and institution accessibility. They need <u>your</u> help and you'll meet engaging people there who observe, think and act in service to the larger senior community!

Another advantage to being a SENIOR, besides having more time, is having your mind available for things other than work. Do you remember how tired your mind was when you got home from work every night, how all you wanted to do was do what you had to and then collapse in front of the tube before you went to sleep? If you're lucky enough to be able to retire, especially in your energetic years, you'll wonder what kinds of things to do to keep your mind vigorous and to expand yourself in exciting ways. Well, worry no more! There are many opportunities in the nearby area to learn just about anything you want, and many of these are earmarked ESPECIALLY FOR SENIORS. For example, **Settlement Music School** offers a SENIORS music program at reduced rates where groups and individuals learn instruments and voice. The **Lively Arts Group** takes trips to Monticello and the Richmond Art Museum, New Orleans as well as to local art spots. They are especially suitable for the SENIOR'S time frame, although they include all ages of art lovers. You can learn folk dancing at any number of small schools, or just go and pick it up where the dances are held, such as the **Art Museum** steps! You'll see many SENIORS there.

One of my favorite groups is the **Friday Forum** put on by Temple Center City as part of the Temple Association for Retired Persons (**TARP**). They have mid-day presentations by notable Philadelphians who then field questions with discussion. A networking-reception period follows. Who will you meet there? People who care about what is going on in the city, people who want to meet <u>other</u> people who care about what is going on in the city. By the way, **TARP** sponsors 60+ fabulous programs of all kinds. You must get their catalog!

There are several excellent resources in town, places where people are very knowledgeable concerning the world of SENIOR activities. One of these is Jackie McClarnin at the **Senior Center of Philadelphia**. Not only does this Center include activities and events for a wide variety of interests (classes in art, dance and computer skills, trips to cultural events and casinos, and on and on), but it is also a clearinghouse of sorts for senior activities in the area. Another general resource is a dandy little paper called *Milestones* which contains useful, interesting information and fun events related to those over 55. It is free and can be found around the city, or you can have it mailed to you.

Remember, too, there are some very fine programs for SENIORS in every neighborhood, located in city-sponsored Senior Centers, churches, synagogues, and community centers. They may provide transportation, meals and assistance in providing information about basic health care and life services for SENIORS. And, very importantly, they help SENIORS link up with other SENIORS for friendship and social activities.

—————— COMMUNITY SERVICE

❑ American Association Of Retired Persons — Volunteer Talent Bank

AARP Fulfillment/EE 0103
1909 K. Street N.W.
Washington, DC 20049

Comments: If you are retired, you can volunteer to help in community service programs through the AARP organization. This national organization for active retirees (50 years and up) can give you leads on where to go to give help.

❑ Foster Grandparents

101 N. Broad Street, 2nd Floor
Philadelphia, PA 19107
(215) 686-9050

Comments: As a mature adult, you can provide cuddling, guidance and companionship to children in day care centers and hospitals. There is a small financial compensation, huge personal reward and lunch.

❑ Retired Senior Volunteer Programs

227 N. 17th Street
Philadelphia, PA 19103
(215) 587-3583

Comments: This local group coordinates volunteer placement for people 55 and over in non-profit organizations, such as schools, libraries and museums (like the Franklin Institute). Transportation and out-of-pocket expenses are reimbursed.

FOLK DANCING

❏ Philadelphia Art Museum (Rocky's Steps)

26th St. & Benjamin Franklin Parkway
Philadelphia, PA
(215) 635-4295

Comments: Great folk dancing on the museum steps in Summer and indoors in Winter. Dancing instruction from 7-8pm with easy and harder dancing afterwards. All ages — from 12 to 75-80 years — attend these dances, with seniors often the experts! All for $3.
Date: Tuesdays   **Time:** 7-10pm

LECTURES

❏ Friday Forum Series

Temple Association For Retired Professionals (TARP)
1616 Walnut Street, Room. 600
Philadelphia, PA 19103
(215) 204-1505

Comments: One of my favorite senior activities. This great program presents an outstanding list of speakers. They include homeless advocate Sr. Mary Scullion, Judge Lisa Richette, movie critic Carrie Rickey. Discussions, coffee cake and conversation!
Date: Fridays   **Time:** 10:30am

MUSIC CLASSES

❏ Daytime Music Program For Older Adults

Settlement Music School
P.O. Box 25120
Philadelphia, PA 19147
(215) 336-0400

Activity Location: *All five branches of Settlement*

Comments: Individuals 60 and over are offered special programs to brush up on musical skills or learn new ones in piano, violin, voice or guitar. Music theory classes and a chamber music group for amateur players are available here.
Date: Monday-Friday   **Time:** 9am-2pm
Cost: For senior citizens, $20/hour or $15/for 3/4 hour for 20 weeks

SENIOR CENTERS
❑ Lutheran Settlement House

1340 Frankford Avenue
Philadelphia, PA 19125
(215) 739-6041

Comments: One example of a large network of senior centers that provides recreation and social activities. These activities include craft making and trips (casinos, Lancaster County, etc.). Many centers also include afternoon meals, volunteer opportunities, and nutrition/health counseling. Transportation to the centers is provided.

❑ Philadelphia Senior Center

509 S. Broad Street
Philadelphia, PA
(215) 546-5879

Comments: This multi-purpose center for people 60+ provides terrific up-to-date classes in computers and other technology, physical fitness and body dynamics, a variety of arts, and dancing of all kinds. Every Thursday there is a local trip, including the casinos once a month, and soon they're going to London! This active and energetic group is booming!
Contact: Jackie McClarnin

TRAVEL
❑ All Adventure Travel

Box 4307
Boulder, CO 80306
(800) 537-4025

Comments: Represents about 40 US and overseas companies specializing in walking, hiking and biking tours. These are listed by level of difficulty and you are matched with a group based on budget, fitness and special interests.

❑ American Association Of Retired People - Travel Experience

> *P.O. Box 7625*
> *Norcross, GA 30091*
> *(800) 927-0111*

Comments: AARP and American Express collaborate to sponsor many types of high quality tours and cruises including walking and train trips in Canada, great river cruises, and fall foliage tours.

❑ Elderhostel

> *75 Federal Street*
> *Boston, MA 02110-1941*
> *(617) 426-8056*

Comments: Elderhostel has an awesome program of thousands of educational adventures in all parts of this country and abroad. Some examples of nearby programs are: in Baltimore, at the Peabody Institute of Music, learning to play the recorder, learning music appreciation and attending live performances; in New Hampshire, a hiking and biology program on the Appalachian Trail. Call for huge catalogs that are fun reading.

❑ Partners For Travel

> *Box 560337*
> *Miami, FL 33256*
> *(800) 866-5565*

Comments: This organization helps single men and women over 40 find travel companions of the same sex. Compatibility is determined by a profile questionnaire. The group also sponsors it's own trips (e.g., Land of Maya).

WORKING VACATIONS

❑ Elderhostel

> *P.O. Box 1959, Dept. AV*
> *Wakefield, MA 01880-5959*
> *(617) 426-7788*

Comments: Elderhostel sponsors project vacations in conjunction with Habitat for Humanity and Oceanic Society Expeditions (dolphins and whales). Write for an Elderhostel service program brochure which lists projects and locations to choose from.

❑ Global Volunteers

> *375 E. Little Canada Road*
> *St. Paul, MN 55117*
> *(800) 487-1074*

Comments: Global offers a special program for Elderhostelers. They are a non-profit group with ongoing projects in Russia, Poland, Indonesia, and other locations abroad and in the U.S. Call for a catalog of volunteer opportunities, such as teaching kids in the Mississippi Delta area.

SENIORS

— NOTES —

Especially for Singles

ART & THEATER
BOOKS
DANCING

DENOMINATIONAL-CATHOLIC
DENOMINATIONAL-JEWISH
DENOMINATIONAL-PROTESTANT

MUSIC
OUTDOORS & SPORTS
SINGLES GROUPS
SOCIAL ISSUES
SPECIAL EVENTS

SINGLES

Sailing on the Chesapeake Bay with Dynamic Diversions.

Professional & Business Singles Network hosts Ruth Harvey workshop on "Great Places to Meet People."

Who doesn't cringe when people talk about the "Singles Scene?" Don't we all just get an unpleasant image of some dark smoky place with very loud rock, where they serve drinks with little parasols and everybody's dressed up in their Hollywood best. These places give off a sort of adolescent feeling — and only those of us who still *look* kind of Hollywood adolescent look forward to it. I suppose it *might* be fun to step back into the excitement of the "promise of Friday night," testing your seduction skills with the best of them. Nothing wrong with that, on an occasional basis.

But isn't the purpose of <u>this</u> directory to offer alternatives to those places? To suggest "Singles Scene" alternatives where you can find all kinds of compatible people who are doing some great things together in the fresh air daylight? These probably would be the people you would enjoy regardless of their marital status.

TRUE, BUT...

There <u>are</u> times when you feel like being with people who are in the same situation with respect to relationships as you are, who are thinking and talking about some of the same socializing issues that you do, and who are <u>available</u> to go to a movie on a Saturday night.

There are times when you as a single person do not feel like being in a situation where everyone else is coupled.

And there are times when you feel like meeting NEW men and women, outside of your usual (terrific) friends, to have fun with. These times may even include adventuresome moments when you feel like looking for candidates for a permanent love relationship. In other words — it's a time for expansion.

Nothing wrong with that.

SINGLES
Forward

Now, **WHERE ARE THEY?**

W*here* are the SINGLE people *you* want to meet? They
could be in that dark smoky place. Never can tell. Problem is,
it's also hard for *you* to tell. I mean, what can you tell about a
person in the dark except that she has pretty legs or he has nice
broad shoulders (No, that's not enough). You might glean
something from the brief shouting discussion you have, or by
how he dances in that cramped space, but probably not much
else. What you likely *can* discern is whether you feel any
animal magnetism, and that's important, but in and of itself it's
usually not a great predictor of a solid ongoing relationship.

When people talk about some deep dark psychological
propensity they have for "choosing the wrong people," I ask
where they meet people. Often they tell me they meet them in
clubs. In such a case, I think the deep dark propensity has more
to do with the deep dark club — where they did the best they
could to choose without knowing about true compatibility
factors. Don't get me wrong: clubbing is a lot of fun. But it's not
a great way to find a mate.

NOT TO WORRY.

There are many groups for SINGLE people (or mostly
single people) that are activity based. Activities — like dancing,
volleyball, sailing, art tours, discussions, and the like, some for
specific populations, like certain age groups, vegetarians,
religious denominations, even people of a particular size and
height. You can't really ask for more, can you?

Some of my favorites include:

The **Professional and Business Singles Network** which
is a large group and sponsors many different types of activities
that include dances, house parties with talks or games, plus
special interest activities like attending art or music events. I
have met interesting people every time I have gone to a PBSN

event, whether it was attractive men or interesting women who would be lots of fun to laugh and pal around with on a Friday night. They send out a booklet-newsletter that details their activities so you can see the events taking place almost every night in different neighborhoods.

Dynamic Diversions, which includes a large component of single people, specializes in great outdoor activities and holds a party every few months. Joe Feisal (the top guy) does a great job of scouting out the adventures and planning first rate trips. The costs are very reasonable: There are activities with food for less than $10!

Single Gourmet, Single Vegetarians, Transitional Dining Club, White Dog Cafe, Ellen Rose, all food things, some of which include discussions (GREAT discussions) about food, current events, or other things. I like food-discussion meetings because it usually insures that you're going to have a good time (eating), and gives you something else to do besides stare at somebody while you talk. Also, there are lots of people there, so you don't have to carry the ball the whole time. It's fun to listen to people talk to *other* people, too — you find out who the good listeners are! Some of these activities are more upscale and expensive than others, so you have alternatives along those lines. Brief mention of a "No Longer" item that I thought was terrific and hope gets reinstated: **The Dining Car**, a very neat diner in the Northeast, had something called "The Friendship Table." If you came in alone and wished to eat with others, they would seat you at a table with other people who came in alone. For people not too shy to be exposed as being alone at dinner, it was a good way to meet people on a casual basis. Won't somebody start it again?

There are many organizations that sponsor special activities for SINGLES who enjoy them and wish to find others who do so too. The **Art Lovers Exchange** holds receptions and programs in art galleries. There are a number of groups which sponsor events for single parents (e.g., **Parents Without Partners**). Their activities may be with and without children, some being discussions of issues of particular interest to single parents. Several organizations include profile information, such as the **Single Booklovers**, even though they have get-togethers as well. Single Booklovers is located nearby but includes a national membership. It is a well-run group, respectable and fun. Another group which connects through profiles is **Concerned Singles** where the emphasis is on meeting others who share your interest (and slant?) in national political issues. For Tennis lovers there is **Tennis for Singles** playing regularly in nearby Princeton. And for those who want to meet other theater going SINGLES, how about **TGIF**, the program co-sponsored by Annenberg Theater and the White Dog Cafe. (That White Dog is a GEM.) There is even a special interest group for SINGLES who love science (**Science Connection**)! If you are wishing for a special focus group and can't find it, maybe you can start it yourself!

Who will you meet there?
The people who go are people who are interested in things, just as you would be if you joined them. It has seemed to me that people who are open to going are clear about their agenda in wanting to meet a group of SINGLE people and perhaps finding a mate.

The 50% divorce rate guarantees that many people are coming and going in SINGLES groups and that means there are many different people attending from week to week. So there are new people to meet, as well as people that you saw last time to pick up a conversation with.

Some people comment on the "desperate losers" who go to SINGLES events, including clubs. I'm never sure why. Are people who are unattached more likely to be losers than people who are attached? In my travels around these organizations I have found terrific people — enthusiastic, gentle, kind, sexy, interesting — all those things — as well as people who were not so appealing. They were like the attached population, only the single people were often a little more engaging. Studies of cross-cultural experience show that you often find what you expect to find. If the only people you find are boring, you might wonder about the signals you're sending, and who you're screening out.

Keep in mind that each person you meet at an activity comes with his connections to all other activities he enjoys. So when you meet others and talk with them about their pleasurable pursuits, you open up a world of possibilities to explore, as specific (Cajun dancing) or as general (Augusta! — an art, music and dance summer camp) as you wish.

One of the golden opportunities that comes with being single is that you can move freely around in the active world. You don't have to get approval for it or coordinate your movements with anyone, and you can explore trying new things with new people using your personal criteria as your only boundary. It's a very exciting time if you invest in yourself!

ART & THEATER

❑ TGIF

Annenberg Center & White Dog Cafe
3680 Walnut Street
Philadelphia, PA
(215) 898-6791

Comments: Performances at Annenberg are followed by meeting the artists and a reception for socializing at the White Dog Cafe. Meet interesting theater goers!
Date: Some Fridays

❑ Art Lovers Exchange

P.O. Box 265
Bensalem, PA 19020-0265
(215) 638-9866

Comments: This group offers an opportunity to meet other single people with an abiding interest in the visual and performing arts. They also go on tours, attend concerts, and give parties. Membership benefits include member profiles.
Cost: $46/Year membership plus cost of events
Contact: Ann Keesee, Director

❑ Artistic Connections

Box 116
Chatham, NJ 07928

Comments: A national organization linking single lovers of the arts: music, theater, film, literature, etc. through member profiles.

❑ Movie Lovers Club

Box 2035
Bala Cynwyd, PA 19004

Comments: I haven't received a response from this group, but it's such a good idea that I've included it anyway. YOU try and see if they still exist, and if they don't, please start another movie lovers group for singles!

BOOKS

❏ Great Books Program

(215) 732-8727

Comments: Small groups discuss our finest literature at a number of locations around the area. Many singles attend and tell me they meet people they really like talking to and feel compatible with.
Contact: Joe Blume

❏ Single Booklovers

Box 117
Gradyville, PA 19039
(215) 358-5049

Comments: A popular, long-standing group of 24 years (!) that serves the needs of cultured singles. Connections are made via member profiles highlighting their favorite books and cultural interests. SB sponsors dinners twice a year, and some members have started book discussion subgroups and get-togethers.
Cost: About $54
Contact: Bob & Ruth Leach

DANCING

❏ Quincy's Sunday Dance

Adam's Mark Hotel
City Avenue & Monument Road
Philadelphia, PA
(215) 581-5000

Comments: Tuesdays and Sundays are great nights for singles (40years+) at Quincy's with a live band on Sundays for Ballroom dancing. Tuesday nights feature a "meeting others via digital messages" event, as well as an after-work buffet.
Date: Sunday   **Time:** 5-10pm

❏ Social Dance Club

Academy Of Social Dance
2011 Sansom Street
Philadelphia, PA
(215) 564-2277

Comments: Dance instruction offered before a DJ hosted dance party — so you can practice what you've just learned! Many but not all are single here. Periodic dance exhibitions by those who have really been involved! Other dance nights also.

Date: Thursdays   **Time:** 9pm-11:45pm
Cost: $10

❏ Singles Dance Party

Jim Scala's "Singles Dance Party"
P.O. Box 254
Media, PA 19063
(215) 358-4773

Activity Location: *The Trolley Stop, Rte 73, Skippack, PA (King Of Prussia Area), (215) 358-4773*

Comments: Long standing group offers dance instruction, food, drinks and socializing. Dances also on Fridays and Sundays in other suburban locations like Media. Call to receive reminder cards of events.

Date: Saturdays   **Time:** 9pm
Cost: $5

❏ Single Set

P.O. Box 24
Lafayette Hills, PA 19444
(215) 938-0978 (Hotline)

Activity Location: *Fiesta Motor Lodge, Rte. 611 & Pa Turnpike, Willow Grove, PA, (215) 659-9300*

Comments: This group sponsors dance parties with Ballroom and line dance lessons to music of live bands. Dancing also takes place in the Northeast (Polish club) on Wednesdays and New Hope (Nottingham Ballroom) on Sundays.

Date: Fridays   **Time:** Evenings

❏ Tower Club Of Philadelphia, Inc.

P.O. Box 7581
Philadelphia, PA 19101
(215) 848-7881

Activity Location: *American Legion Post #372, Martin Avenue & Marlboro Road, Cherry Hill, NJ.*

Comments: Dancing is only one activity sponsored by this social club for tall men (over 6'2") and women (5'10"+). A group not just for singles, they have cultural events, house parties, weekend events, dining and dancing, trips and tours.

Date: 4th Friday   **Time**: 9pm-1am
Cost: No cover, cash bar

❏ Tuesday Night Square-Dance Guild

St. Mary's Church
39th & Locust Walk (U. of P. campus)
Philadelphia, PA
(215) 386-3916

Comments: This group has been dancing for years and people love it. No partner or experience needed. Many singles but open to everyone.

Date: 2nd Tuesday/month   **Time**: 7:30-10:30pm
Cost: $5

—— DENOMINATIONAL-CATHOLIC

❏ Epsilon Catholic Young Adult Club

Box 6632
Philadelphia, PA 19149
(215) 288-6814

Comments: Open to Catholic singles ages 21-40 to join their diverse range of activities. They go on outdoor high adventures, canoeing and hiking, as well as bowling and volleyball events. They sponsor dances jointly with other groups (like CAC), including square dances, dinner nights and club nights. Lots is happening in this social community!

Date: Tuesday night meetings
Contact: Vern Rose

SINGLES

❏ Community Singles Of Lady of Good Counsel

P.O. Box 991
Southhampton, PA
(215) 822-1972

Activity Location: *Our Lady Of Good Counsel Church, 611 Knowles Avenue, Southampton, PA, (215) 357-3553*

Comments: A lively singles group that enjoys from 7-10 activities a month. Included are things like volleyball, miniature golf, suppers, biking, softball, trips to the Phillies, pool parties, theme parties. Interested yet? Ages 21 to 45 years, and you don't have to be Catholic. Call to get a newsletter of events!
Contact: Terri Oxman

❏ Catholic Alumni Club Of Philadelphia (CAC)

Box 53287
Philadelphia, PA 19105
(215) 649-9476

Comments: Single Catholic professionals (and associates) ages 25 and over for social activities. Calling the number above will connect you with Joy McCartney, Coordinator for Catholic Young Adult and Singles Groups in Philadelphia.

DENOMINATIONAL-JEWISH

❏ Liberty Chapter Ort

Temple Beth Ami
9201 Old Bustleton Avenue
Philadelphia, PA
(215) 673-6613

Comments: Social activities for a mature singles group (45+) and over to benefit ORT. They sponsor day trips to Atlantic City, New York City (for shows), and others.
Contact: Ruth

❑ Singles Forum Of Temple Sinai

Temple Sinai
Limekiln Pike & Dillon Road
Dresher, PA
(215) 624-6973

Comments: Jewish singles club ages 21-50. They arrange dances in local clubs, outdoor trips (like tubing! and amusement parks) and arts activities. Call for schedule.
Contact: Barbara

❑ Hillel of Greater Philadelphia

(215) 769-1175

Comments: The Jewish student community on campus and in your neighborhood. They sponsor a wide variety of programs for every interest, including white water rafting, parties, dances, holiday celebrations, and Shabbat dinners. For graduate and professional students, call 898-6451.

❑ Beth Shalom Singles

Beth Shalom Congregation
Old York & Foxcroft Roads
Elkins Park, PA
(215) 887-1350

Comments: Jewish Club for ages 21-35.

❑ Jewish Professional & Business Singles

Box 1355
Bensalem, PA 19020
(215) 752-2179

Comments: Discussions, trips (dance weekends with Umbrella Singles in the Poconos), house and swim parties, and dances in local clubs (in reserved areas) for singles 35 years and over.
Cost: Only activity fees
Contact: Loretta

DENOMINATIONAL-PROTESTANT

❑ Vision/20 Something/Focus

Network of Church Of The Savior
Church Of The Savior
651 N. Wayne Avenue
Wayne, PA
(215) 964-8906

Comments: Three singles groups for different ages hold discussions about Christian issues, being single, etc. as well as a wide variety of social activities such as mystery dinners, hayrides, and trips. Visitors can check out the monthly coffeehouse. Call for info.

FOOD

❑ Dining Group

Single Vegetarians Friendship Network
P.O. Box 24353
Philadelphia, PA 19120
(215) 276-3198

Comments: Join other single vegetarians for many events at Veggie restaurants in the area. They are part of the Vegetarians of Philadelphia organization.

❑ The Single Gourmet

100 E. Highway 34, Suite 145
Matawan, NJ 07747
(215) 238-1448

Comments: Eat in fine quality restaurants with this group of socializing singles which meets as often as 4 nights a week. The restaurants are diverse in type and price, and evenings may include parties and dancing. The group travels together as well.
Cost: Membership $100/year; $40-$60/evening
Contact: Florence Weltmen

❑ Transitional Dining Club (TDC)

P.O. Box 238
Broomall, PA 19008
(215) 543-7075 Hotline

Activity Location: *Local "upscale" restaurants, social dining and dancing clubs*

Comments: Dining club for singles. You can check out this group before joining with a trial membership including a full course dinner with TDC. Newsletter.

MUSIC

❑ Classical Music Lovers' Exchange

Box 31
Pelham, NY 10803
(800) 233-CMLS

Comments: Nationwide group brings together unattached music lovers to share musical interests via brief compatibility profile. Newsletter.
Cost: Membership $65 for 6 months

❑ Musical Intros

P.O. Box 1140
Valley Forge, PA 19482-1140

Comments: A way to meet musically oriented singles through biographical descriptions.
Cost: $25 for 3 months

———————— OUTDOORS & SPORTS

❑ Dynamic Diversions

P.O. Box 42775
Philadelphia, PA 19101
(215) 849-9944

Comments: "Recreation for the Discriminating Individual," states the newsletter. This great group organizes barbecues, hiking, canoeing, parties, and many other outdoor (and some indoor) activities. Well-run and very nice people here, who are mostly, but not all single.
Cost: $15/first year, plus fee for activity
Contact: Joe Feisal

❑ Mixed Doubles For Singles

5072 Beech Court
Monmouth Junction, NJ 08852
(908) 274-2019

Activity Location: *Princeton Indoor Tennis Center, Princeton Heightstown Road, Princeton, NJ*

Comments: Play tennis and have fun with other single tennis players. Two to three hours of play, good food and new friends. Intermediate and advanced level players welcome.
Date: Monthly   **Time**: 7pm
Cost: $25/party
Contact: Sandy Burns

❑ Science Connection

P.O. Box 188
Youngstown, NY 14174
(800) 667-5179

Comments: A North America-wide singles network for science and nature enthusiasts. Ages 20's to 80's.

❏ Sierra Singles

> *P.O. Box 2242*
> *Doylestown, PA 18901*
> *(215) 297-8575*

Comments: A singles subgroup of the Bucks County Sierra Club. Nice variety of activities including dinners, day hikes, and other socializing activities like swing dancing! All ages.

❏ Singles On Sailboats (SOS)

> *Bay Ridge Inn*
> *Annapolis, MD*
> *(410) 997-1595*

Comments: Sailing activities and brunch for people truly interested in sailing.
Date: Sundays
Cost: About $15 for brunch

SINGLES GROUPS

❏ At Large

> *1084201 Neshaminy Boulevard, Suite 231*
> *Bensalem, PA 19020*
> *(215) 552-8701*

Comments: Discussions, parties, trips and a newsletter listing many events for people of size.
Cost: Send SASE for free information

SINGLES

❑ Connections

Unitarian Church
401 N. Kings Highway
Cherry Hill, NJ
(609) 667-7688

Comments: Meets for dinner, good speaker/discussions, and dancing every Thursday. Discussion topics include: "Developing Your Creativity," "Intimate companions," and "Parapsychology." Call hotline for upcoming events. Many outdoor activities also.
Date: Thursdays   **Time**: 7:30-11:40pm
Contact: Joel

❑ Northeast Singles Club

Knights Of Columbus Hall
3300 Knorr Street
Philadelphia, PA
(215) 535-1115

Comments: This group for single people ages 40 and over sponsors a dance and social event, and a regular card game. Call to find out how to receive their monthly newsletter.
Date: First Sunday/month   **Time**: 7:30pm

❑ Parents Without Partners

Box 11455
Philadelphia, PA
(215) 688-4829 (King of Prussia) or 332-0622 (NE Phila.)

Comments: A <u>major</u> organization that sponsors excellent social events and large dances in many Philadelphia locations for single parents. All ages of great single people attend their activities.

❏ Professional and Business Single Network

> *Box 404*
> *Paoli, PA 19301*
> *(215) 353-4624*

Comments: This group sponsors a large number of quality activities. A large Sunday night dance in King of Prussia is just one of many dances given by PBSN preceded by an interesting speaker. They also give house parties, game nights, salon evenings and other creative activities. Some events are for singles under 35 years. Call for large catalog of events — there's something almost every night!
Contact: Ralph Israel

❏ Single Parents Society

> *Catholic War Veterans Post*
> *71st Street & Elmwood Avenue*
> *Philadelphia, PA*
> *(215) 928-9433*

Comments: This is one of eight chapters of this group for all ages in the Delaware Valley. SPS sponsors many activities including excursions, educational programs, buffets, dancing to live bands, and events which include children. Monthly newsletter listing events of all chapters.
Date: Fridays   **Time**: 9-12pm

❏ Singles Scene

> *Unitarian Universalist Church*
> *Stenton Avenue & Gorgas Lane*
> *Philadelphia, PA*
> *(215) 224-4217*

Comments: Socializing, discussions and dancing are all happening at this dynamic group. At 7:30pm: casual socializing in cafe setting; at 9pm: discussion groups with themes like "Tax Tips for Singles," or different types of dance lessons — and at 10pm: dancing!
Date: Saturdays   **Time**: 7:30pm-12:30am
Cost: About $6
Contact: Betty

SINGLES

Singles Groups • Social Issues • Special Events

❑ Weekenders

Beck-O-Neill-Strouse Funeral Home
7400 New Falls Road
Levittown, PA
(215) 946-7603

Comments: Primarily single women ages 40+ (but open to all) doing all kinds of great activities, such as hayrides, trips, and book readings. Newsletter available.
Date: 2nd Saturday/month   **Time**: 7pm
Cost: Reasonable fees for events
Contact: Kathleen

SOCIAL ISSUES
❑ Concerned Singles Newsletter

Box 555
N. Stockbridge, MA 01262

Comments: Nationwide group since 1984 links singles of all ages concerned about social justice, environment, etc. Free sample.

SPECIAL EVENTS
❑ Annual Singles Charity Party

Academy Of Natural Sciences
1900 Benjamin Franklin Parkway
Philadelphia, PA
(215) 830-0587

Comments: Entertainment, karaoke, dancing, prizes, free food and drink. Come in sneakers and jeans. Benefits Breast Health Institute. Great fun!
Date: Annual in January
Contact: Ellis Toder

❑ Wear Your Heart On Your Sleeve

Ritz-Carlton
17th & Chestnut Streets
Philadelphia, PA
(215) 563-1600 Ext 450

Comments: Annual Valentine's Day singles dinner where men move from table to table between courses and mingle with the gals. Sounds like fun! Reservations required.
Date: Valentine's Day
Cost: $60

❑ Annual Singles Symposium

Delaware County Community College
Media, PA 19063
(215) 359-5025

Comments: Information tables, panels and workshops such as: "The Art of Conversation," "Breaking Up But Not Breaking Down," etc. While you're exploring singles resources, it's a great place to meet people and network with other singles!
Date: Annual in November   **Time:** 8:30am-4pm

SINGLES

— NOTES —

CLASSES/WORKSHOPS

CLUBS

DISCUSSIONS/PROGRAMS

PERFORMING

PERFORMING—INFORMAL

OPEN STAGE

PERFORMING/CLASSES

PLAYREADING

STORYTELLING

Director A. Posner (right) leads Shakespeare class, part of the ACT Program at Arden Theater Company. Photo by Sue Winge.

People who go on and on about the GREAT THEATER ACTIVITIES in New York give me a pain because there are some really exciting THEATER opportunities right under our noses in Philly!

If you're new to THEATER and you're the type of person who likes to *know* what you're doing, there are a number of excellent schools that teach theater skills. Some of these are connected to well established theaters such as the **Wilma**, **Hedgerow**, **Arden**, **Freedom** and the **Walnut Street** Theaters. Classes also can be found in schools that teach a variety of arts, including theater arts with performing opportunities, like **Allen's Lane Art Center**, **Cheltenham Art Center** and the **University of the Arts**. By the way, there are two theaters that are especially for African Americans: the **Bushfire** and the **Freedom** Theaters, where there is some incredible theater happening. These learning opportunities vary in price, scholarship opportunities and theater-acting philosophy, but they are all solid theater programs. You can collect catalogs, ask around, or call the company and ask them to discuss their program with you to find the best theater experience for you. Even better, go to some performances of the theater groups you're considering hooking up with and see for yourself the quality of their productions. If you're not new, if you're a seasoned performer/set designer etc., you can look under "Auditions" in the *Welcomat* (after Events) or the *Inquirer* (in the Entertainment Section) and go for it! Better yet, subscribe to **STAGE** newsletter which lists Auditions and Theater Events in the area for several months ahead.

Sprinkled throughout the neighborhoods of the city are about half a dozen small theaters that regularly present fine quality plays. Theaters like The **Old Academy Players**, **Stagecrafters**, and the **Society Hill Playhouse** are examples. Although some require more theater skills than others, all invite both beginners and experienced people to be a part of their productions in many roles. Call them to ask about your particular talents and aspirations.

If you'd like a bit of theater experience that is more informal, if you just want a chance to *see* if "doing" theater is *your thing*, you have many opportunities to be involved. For example, one fine group is the **Drama Group** operating in the Methodist Church in Germantown which puts on regular productions and warmly invite all interested to come around. Another is the **Actors Center** in the Bourse which sponsors all kinds of theater arts activities, like cabaret and comedy, play readings; also, an Open Mike Night for recovering people. One of my favorites is at the **Red Brick Theater** where they do "script in hand" readings of new plays on Tuesday evenings. Good for the playwright getting a dry run of her play <u>and</u> a valuable opportunity for the aspiring acting professionals to show off their talent! Is that excellent or what?!

Coming from a more playful slant, you could take a class in **Storytelling**, the oldest form of acting, with **Robin Moore**. It connects the world of drama to the drama in your heart, besides endearing you to anyone who is lucky enough to hear you. And again, we have the **Eastern Cooperative Recreational School**, where you can do dramatics of all kinds in weekend or week-long workshops. The **Bothy Club** is an open stage located at the Mermaid Inn where many people do stand-up acting, singing and comedy bits for fresh and exuberant audiences. And if you want to find a class that is especially reasonable, the City's **Department of Recreation** has dramatics programs free of charge!

The great thing about doing theater things is that there are so many ways to be involved. You can take classes and then perform (or not) in major theaters, or be a part of a small group of players. You can be involved in one of the many types of production activities, like set design, costume making, music playing, script work, lighting, ushering/ticket taking, promotion and a number of supportive jobs. Making a play performance happen is the result of many peoples' work, and the experience of working *together* on such a cooperative venture is an exciting way to network. Another nice thing about it is that it is a time-limited commitment. You are part of an ongoing group that agrees to meet and work together to put this thing together but you are only committed for the life of the play, usually about 6-8 weeks. If you can't stand it, you can gracefully leave after that, or you can try it again and leave after the next 6-8 week production, etc. I don't mean to be negative — you'll probably love it and stay in the theater for years, meeting more and more sophisticated and creative people — but it's nice to know that you can try things to see how they work for you.

But maybe your interest in theater has more to do with being an active audience, learning the lessons of wisdom from the great playwrights, and you'd like to find others who are interested in a theater-goers network. Lucky you! The **Plays and Players Club** sponsors terrific activities for theater lovers like dinners, receptions, and discussions with playwrights. Also, the **White Dog Cafe** has hooked up with **Movement International Theater** for theater and fine dinner-conversation evenings for those who want to get together and talk about the performances, as well as other interesting topics. There are also discussions, receptions and meet-the-playwright opportunities at the **Annenberg Center** and **Painted Bride** — where you not only meet the authors and performers but each other as well.

As I said, Philadelphia offers many wonderful interactive theater events — you need only to reach for it!

—————————— CLASSES/WORKSHOPS
❑ Cheltenham School For Arts

> *439 Ashbourne Road*
> *Cheltenham, PA*
> *(215) 379-4660*

Comments: This all-around arts center offers a variety of classes in theater arts, such as "Introduction to Performing," "Advanced Acting," and "Scene Study." Occasionally they use experienced local actors in their productions.

❑ Performance Class

> *Motion Studios*
> *7140 Germantown Avenue (Mt. Airy)*
> *Philadelphia, PA 19119*
> *(215) 242-0660*

Comments: Terrific ambiance in this studio specializing in fitness, dance and theater arts such as acting, script writing, voice, and set and costume design. Free parking on premises.
Cost: Very reasonable

❑ Sharing Dreams

> *Phoenix Power And Light Co, Inc.*
> *Drawer 5665*
> *Virginia Beach, VA 23455*

Comments: Annual week-long conference in Virginia doing clowning, dance, mime, storytelling, and puppetry. PPLC is a non profit group for the arts in religion and community. A theater getaway!
Date: Annual in July

❑ University City Arts League

> *4226 Spruce Street*
> *Philadelphia, PA 19104*
> *(215) 382-7811*

Comments: Very reasonable classes in all the arts, including theater arts. Check out the theater workshop for doing acting, singing, production, and dance.

THEATER

Classes/Workshops • Club

❏ University Of The Arts

309 S. Broad Street
Philadelphia, PA
(215) 875-2232

Comments: Major excellent classes at this college, which includes seminars and workshops in theater for non-matriculating students like you and me.

CLUB

❏ Plays & Players

1714 Delancey Place
Philadelphia, PA 19103
(215) 735-0630

Comments: Plays and Players Club has Friday night receptions and discussions, parties, brunches, theater dinners — and much socializing! Also workshops, newsletter, and auditions.

❏ The Lively Arts Group

117 S. 17th St, Suite 300
Philadelphia, PA 19103
(215) 567-3339

Comments: This non-profit educational group for arts appreciation sponsors excellent local and extended trips to museums and shows, including the Museum of Modern Art (NYC), Longwood Gardens, the Philadelphia Orchestra, and the Kennedy Center (DC).
Contact: Naomi Klein

———— DISCUSSIONS/PROGRAMS
❏ Philadelphia Festival Theater-New Plays

3900 Chestnut Street
Philadelphia, PA 19104
(215) 222-5000

Activity Location: *Annenberg Center-Harold Prince, 3680 Walnut Street,*
Philadelphia, PA 19104, (215) 222-5000

Comments: Sponsors play readings of new plays for $5! Also, sub-
scribers have curtain call discussions with playwrights, actors and
directors.

❏ Philadelphia Drama Guild

100 N. 17th Street
Philadelphia, PA 19103
(215) 563-Play

Activity Location: *Zellerbach Theatre/Annenberg Center, 3680*
Walnut Street, Philadelphia, PA 19104

Comments: Subscriber benefits include discussions with the cast and
a luncheon series with theatrical speakers before the play.

❏ The Painted Bride

230 Vine Street
Philadelphia, PA 19106
(215) 925-9914

Comments: The Painted Bride is a creative forum for many Philadelphia communities of performing arts showcasing local artists. They
host discussions, lectures, cultural films, music and art.

❑ Fools Feast

White Dog Cafe & Movement Theater International
3420 Sansom Street
Philadelphia, PA
(215) 386-9224/382-0600

Comments: The White Dog Cafe and MTI have put together various evenings that include a show with a discussion after. The White Dog sponsors <u>many</u> discussion groups about theater, the arts, and contemporary issues. Call for info and newsletter.

PERFORMING

❑ Allens Lane Cafe Theater

Allens Lane Art Center
Allens Lane & McCallum Streets
Philadelphia, PA 19119
(215) 248-0546

Comments: An excellent amateur theater. Open auditions.

❑ Hedgerow Theater

64 Rose Valley Road
Moylan, PA
(215) 565-8286

Comments: This terrific theater allows auditions from the community, but you might want to take one of their classes first! They teach acting, scene study, and performance at all levels of experience. You can volunteer for all aspects of theater including public relations, sewing costumes, and the many facets of scene production and artistry.

❑ Old Academy Players

3544 Indian Queen Lane
Philadelphia, PA (East Falls)
(215) 485-9929

Comments: This group encourages non-professionals to be involved in all phases of theater production.
Contact: Mary Maguire, Chairwoman, Production Committee

❏ Playworks Theater Company

623 South Street
Philadelphia, PA 19147
(215) 592-8393

Comments: A small company seeks volunteers to be involved in all aspects of running the theater: house and stage managers, taking tickets, ushers, office people. Great opportunities behind the scenes!

❏ Stagecrafters

8130 Germantown Avenue
Philadelphia, PA
(215) 247-8881

Comments: Open auditions held for performances in this theater in Chestnut Hill. Opportunities to be involved in many ways here.

❏ The Actors Center Theater Company

Bourse Building
5th & Market Streets
Philadelphia, PA
(215) 925-6400

Comments: Great eclectic theater group that has opportunities for all performing arts: cabaret/comedy, art on the walls, and plays. Aspiring artists and those who just want to volunteer are welcome. On Mondays they host Open Mike for Artists for Recovery. "Best of Philly, '94!"
Contact: Joe Koroly

❏ The Drama Group

First United Methodist Church of Germantown
6023 Germantown Avenue
Philadelphia, PA 19144
(215) 844-0724

Comments: Small, friendly, supportive group who make theater happen. Beginners and experienced performers are both welcome to be involved in all parts of production.
Contact: Robert Bauer

THEATER
Performing—Informal

PERFORMING—INFORMAL

☐ Open Circle

The Mermaid Inn
7673 Germantown Avenue
Philadelphia, PA (Chestnut Hill)
(215) 247-9797

Comments: Open Circle is an informal open performing event for singers, musicians, and actors. Long standing group but new people welcome. Comfortable ambiance.
Date: 2nd & 4th Thursday   **Time**: 8:30pm

☐ Formal Dramatics/Environmental Theater

City Department of Recreation: Cultural Events
Northeast and Northwest Philadelphia locations
(215) 685-0151

Comments: Program of adult dramatics, working on entire productions. In the Northwest: Water Tower in Chestnut Hill. In the Northeast: Longcrest Center.
Date: Fall and winter
Cost: Free
Contact: Edgar Brown

☐ Eastern Cooperative Recreational School

480 Valley Road, Apt C-7
Montclair, NJ 07043
(215) 729-6738 (local contact)

Activity Location: *Camp Onas, Ottsville, PA*

Comments: The Spring Camping Weekend is one of many events sponsored by ECRS. You'll have a chance to try many activities in a supportive atmosphere, including acting in small scenes, storytelling, dancing, singing and more. They hold a week-long camp, too!
Date: Annual in June
Cost: Very reasonable and scholarships
Contact: Karen Wisnia (PA contact)

OPEN STAGE

❑ Bothy Club

Mermaid Inn
7673 Germantown Avenue
Philadelphia, PA (Chestnut Hill)
(215) 247-9797

Comments: This is a long standing open stage event. You can get up and strut your stuff and see how it fares! Stand up, impromptu performing.

Date: Mondays   **Time:** 7:30pm
Contact: Tom Gala

PERFORMING/ CLASSES

❑ Bushfire Theater

52nd & Locust Street
Philadelphia, PA (West Philadelphia)
(215) 747-9230

Comments: Classes for African-American writers and performers. Subscribers may attend free readings and workshops of new plays. The Writers Cafe has workshops, while the Cafe-Theater sponsors jazz, blues, etc.

Freedom Theatre

Heritage House
1346 N. Broad Street
Philadelphia, PA 19121
(215) 765-2793

Comments: Philadelphia's oldest black theater sponsors open casting for plays and study programs.

❏ Society Hill Playhouse

507 S. 8th Street
Philadelphia, PA 19147
(215) 923-0210

Comments: Open auditions for productions in this fine theater. Acting classes also.

❏ The Arden Theatre Company

St. Stephen's Alley Performing Arts Center
10th & Ludlow Streets
Philadelphia, PA
(215) 829-8900

Comments: Professional classes and workshops offered in acting, voice, play writing, dance, etc. Work-study available, helping with production.
Cost: $150-$175/8-week class

❏ Walnut Street Theatre School

Walnut Street Theatre Building
9th & Walnut Streets
Philadelphia, PA 19107
(215) 574-3550 Ext. 566

Comments: Comprehensive theatrical training center with classes for all levels of experience. Acting, directing, play writing, singing, movement, and more are available.
Cost: 12-week classes approximately $230/class

❏ Wilma Theater School

Wilma Theater Studio
2030 Sansom Street
Philadelphia, PA
(215) 963-0249

Comments: Classes using the Gordon Phillips method. Students audition for performances. Occasional open auditions.
Cost: 8 weeks, between $100-$200

PLAY READING

❑ Theater Center Philadelphia

Red Brick Theater
over Montserrat Restaurant
623 South Street
Philadelphia, PA
(215) 336-3869

Comments: Playwrights and actor/readers welcome to perform "script in hand" on the spot readings! Productions also.
Date: Tuesday   **Time**: 8pm
Cost: $3

❑ Toastmasters International

Philadelphia School of Textile & Science
School House Lane & Henry Avenue
Philadelphia, PA 19144 (East Falls)
(215) 951-2902

Comments: Learn to speak effectively in front of groups with a chance to practice what you learn — and have fun doing it! This is the Northwest Branch of Toastmasters which also meets in Center City.
Contact: Lorrie Distefano

STORYTELLING

❑ Awakening The Hidden Storyteller

Box 81
Springhouse, PA 19477
(215) 646-2150

Comments: Workshops by Robin Moore, a master storyteller who uses special techniques to assist people to create spoken and written stories. Mr. Moore also runs classes at Cheltenham and the University of Pennsylvania General Studies Program.
Contact: Robin Moore

Vacations

BIKING

BOATING

DANCE & MUSIC

ENVIRONMENTAL TRIPS

INTERNATIONAL CONTACT

OUTDOORS

PERSONAL GROWTH

SENIORS

SINGLES

SPORTS

UNIVERSITY VACATIONS

VACATIONS

Dynamic Diversions group admires view at Hawk Mountain Sanctuary.

Elderhostelers grading maple sugar with the Appalachian Mountain Club, NH. Photo by Rob Burbank.

VACATIONS

This is the chapter that is <u>not</u> about Philadelphia. By definition, it is about places away from Philadelphia — VACATION places, where Philadelphians can meet compatible people. What distinguishes <u>these</u> VACATIONS is that they are not lying-on-the-beach trips. They are active, learning, collaborating, building, moving experiences. And at the heart of them all is interaction with others.

The friends you make building a soft bridge in Ecuador can support a social life connection in Philadelphia. First off, you might maintain phone (or on-line) contact with the people you met on your trip or have an occasional reunion. You might even arrange to go on VACATION with them next year. Secondly, you could be entering into an interest group/network that extends to Philadelphia and meet others, not on the trip, who share that interest. At the very least, you will be "out there," meeting compatible people, and learning people skills you would miss if you went on a safe vacation to the beach (again) with your friends.

So where to go??

We can start with several premier groups that specialize in outdoorsy Adventurous experiences in small groups that usually have some kind of learning designed into the experience. **REI**, out of the beautiful Pacific Northwest, has trips all over the U.S. and abroad. They backpack, kayak, mountain climb and engage in other rigorous activities in various *gorgeous* locations. The **Sierra Club** has similar activities but includes programs that educate about our natural resources, such as a weekend expedition to watch bald eagles. **Outward Bound**, for all ages, has similar activities but plans a deliberate personal growth component. You build personal confidence, group skills, or learn special competencies while you to go on a wilderness expedition in the Rio Grande, for example. **EarthWatch** recruits volunteers to assist scientists in field operations, from monitoring mountain lion populations to excavating 26,000-year-old mammoth bones in South Dakota. The catalogs for all four groups will knock you out with dynamic interactive adventures in incredible places!

In the Outdoors arena are numerous programs specializing in one or another type of activity. Some examples: biking and hiking in Vermont, where you stay in a different country inn each night (**Cycle & Walking Inn Vermont**), biking around the Chesapeake (or New Hope), white-water rafting on the Lehigh River, sailing on a schooner on the Chesapeake Bay (**Eastern Bay Charter**) or out of Mystic Conn., and orienteering in state parks around the country. If you want more organized sports activities, you could try **New England Hiking & Tennis** with a tennis camp in Swarthmore and New Hampshire, or a variety of golf camps along the Eastern seaboard. The **Appalachian Mountain Club** offers great hiking trips on beautiful and well-established trails in those lovely mountains.

There are outstanding music and art camps where you can dance, sing, play instruments, make instruments, do drama and other performing and visual arts activities. In Massachusetts, **Pinewoods** specializes in dancing, and sponsors several types of dancing each week. **Augusta!** is a camp in West Virginia which organizes various weeks around a theme. For instance, you learn about Bluegrass dancing, music playing and singing during Bluegrass week. Closer to home, **Omega** in upstate New York, sponsors hundreds of workshops all year, mostly in summer. They all look like great fun and tremendous learning as well. Because there's such a great variety of programs, there is truly something for everyone, with very enthusiastic reviews from all the participants I've talked to.

VACATIONS

Some VACATIONS, trips and groups, are organized for specific types of travelers: women, singles, seniors. For seniors, **Elderhostel** is a very large and established program offering literally thousands of exploratory trips. The quality is outstanding and people report the trips have changed their lives. Programs include the "Fine Arts of Britain," "The Ceramics of Mexico," and "The Volcanoes of Costa Rica," and many others in the United States. Single people can be involved in environmental forays with the **Sierra Club**, learn a sport like tennis, or take part in one of the many **Club Med** groups where all the participants are also single.

And, lastly, if you love <u>learning</u> VACATIONS, you can go back to school! There are "camps" located on university campuses that offer reasonable accommodations with imaginative courses in just about everything, taught by university personnel. My favorite is the **Asimov Seminar at Rensselaerville Institute** where participants build and live in an Asimov-based conceptual world, led by Asimov experts. What an amazing week that must be!

Some Notes of Encouragement

VACATIONS are very special times to develop exciting <u>new interests</u>. This is true for a number of reasons. You have more open time and energy, and less general stress. Also, you have the chance to learn something and get involved doing it for a concentrated period of time without the distractions of routine life demands. Further, you may be doing these things in new, exciting and beautiful settings—settings that can expand your perspective and stimulate your interest. To top it off, since being actively engaged in something new is often quite restorative, you could return from your vacation quite refreshed!

VACATIONS are also a great time to take a fresh look at your self and your life. There is something liberating about not being home where you are bound by your regular surroundings and your usual ways of being. Things often look different when you're away. They take on a different cast. Psychologists call this changing your "set." It's an expanding experience causing you to widen your perspective. Being away is also a great time to experiment with your usual ways of <u>behaving</u>. For example: you can get up earlier and think or meditate. When you meet others at breakfast you can talk quietly and peacefully about the lovely view (instead of how you usually act in the morning...!). Or you can <u>risk</u> more than you usually do at home (where people will remember forever if you fall on your face) and talk more (or less), take leadership (or following) roles, ask someone that interests you to lunch (or let them ask you) — something different! It's a chance to extend your experiences, to try on other ways to be with yourself and others. Fun. Interesting. Watch yourself. How do you like it? If you don't, you can go back to your usual ways when you get home and not confuse your friends!

To expand your information about the specific places you might want to go, a <u>great</u> place to get information about active vacations is travel book stores, such as **Way To Go** on Main Street in Manayunk, The people who own it and work there are both helpful and knowledgeable. Have a great trip!

BIKING

❏ Country Cycling Tours

140 W. 83rd Street
New York, NY 10024
(212) 874-5151

Comments: This group has cycling trips all over the U.S. (and abroad), including some local excursions on the Chesapeake Bay and around New Hope. You can go for a day or several weeks. Trips are for all ages and include leisure exploration of the region, shops and all.

❏ Cycle Inn

(802) 228-8799

Activity Location: *Combes Family Inn, Vermont*

Comments: Cycle Inn is a group of Vermont inn-keepers who help you plan bike and hike trips. They make reservations, transport your luggage and provide you with rented bikes if you need them.

❏ Mountain Bike School

Mount Snow Resort
Mount Snow, VT 05356
(800) 451-4211

Comments: While learning the best way to maneuver a mountain bike, you might as well be in gorgeous Vermont! You need to be reasonably fit to do this exciting vacation. Bike rentals available.

❏ Vermont Bicycle Touring

(802) 453-4811

Comments: From about 1972, this group has been planning trips in the U.S. and internationally, for all ages and fitness levels. Great descriptive catalogs to help you plan your trip.
Contact: Raymond

BOATING

❑ Adirondack River Outfitters

> Box 649
> Old Forge, NY 13420
> (315) 369-3536

Activity Location: *Hudson, Moose, Black Rivers*

Comments: Full participation white water rafting trip where equipment is provided. Rich folklore is offered by licensed guides from the area.
Date: April-October
Cost: $10-$85/day group; $100-$150/individual

❑ Craftsbury Sculling Center

> Box 31
> Craftsbury Common, VT 05827
> (800) 729-7751

Comments: All ages and abilities learn sculling and sweep rowing on a sensationally scenic lake that shines like a huge sheet of mica. Craftsbury also has fly fishing, nature walks and birding, horseback riding and other wonderful programs.

❑ Delaware River Canoe Association

> Kittatinny Canoes
> Dingman's Ferry, PA 18328
> (717) 828-2700

Activity Location: *Variety of Northern Delaware River locations*

Comments: Rafting and boating classes held on the second weekend of every month. They also rent canoes and offer tubing, kayaking and rafting trips.
Date: Spring/summer/fall

❑ Set Sail On The Schooner "Farewell"

Eastern Bay Charter
P.O. Box 452
St. Michaels, MD 21663
(301) 886-2489

Comments: Daysails on board a 40-foot traditional schooner. Licensed captain with daily sails on the gorgeous and historical Chesapeake Bay. Maximum 6 people.
Cost: $35/Person

❑ Out Of Mystic Schooner Cruises

Box 487
Mystic, CT 06355
(800) 243-0416

Comments: Fantastic windjammer sailing out of Old Mystic, Conn. Private cabins, tile heads with showers and hearty meals. This sweet schooner is 125' long, 26' wide. You can settle in and relax or you can get involved in helping sail the ship!
Cost: About $250 for 2 days/nights

❑ Outback Expeditions

Mexico/ Alaska / Washington State
Box 16343
Seattle, WA 98116
(206) 932-7012

Comments: Sea kayak and land tour adventure packages. Professionally guided one- to 11-day kayak trips that encourage a feeling of oneness with the water and the natural surroundings. Gear and three healthy meals are provided; you bring personals.

DANCE & MUSIC

❏ Augusta!

Augusta Heritage Center
c/o Davis & Elkins College
100 Sycamore Street
Elkins, WV 06241-3996
(304) 636-1903

Comments: Great summer camp which specializes in different types of music, dance, and crafts each week. They have Blues Week, Native American Week, Irish Week, Bluegrass Week, Cajun Week, etc. So you can dance and play or soak up music all week!
Date: Weekly in July and August

❏ The Country Dance & Song Society

Pinewoods Camp
17 New South Street
Northampton, MA 01060
(413) 584-9913

Comments: Long standing camp with weekly programs: Early Music Week, American Dance And Music Week, English and American Dance Week, Folk Music Week, etc. People say it's a terrific experience — and they return year after year.
Date: Weekly in July and August

ENVIRONMENTAL TRIPS

❏ Appalachian Mountain Club

8412 Widner Road
Wyndmoor, PA
(215) 836-2497

Comments: People get out there and walk, hike, and climb. Moreover, volunteers contribute to the Earth by doing research and by helping develop policy to impact environmental legislation.
Cost: $40/Adult

❑ Whale-Watching Trips

> *Bucks County Community College, Biology Department*
> *Swamp Road*
> *Newtown, PA 18940*
> *(215) 968-8409*

Comments: Periodic whale-watching trips to Provincetown, Mass. Half-day guided watch cruises, plus guided birding tours and three days at a Holiday Inn.
Cost: Very reasonable
Contact: Eugene Ferri

❑ Earthwatch

> *Box 403*
> *Watertown, MA 02172*
> *(617) 926-8200*

Comments: Earthwatch sponsors programs of volunteers and scientists working together to solve significant environmental problems. Projects include trips to study Israeli desert floods, humpbacks off Hawaii, an ancient Iberian village, and a Bahamian reef survey to name a few. Great catalog.
Cost: You pay something toward your expenses.

❑ Hiking

> *New England Hiking & Tennis Holidays*
> *Box 1648*
> *North Conway, NH 03860*
> *(800) 869-0949*

Comments: Tennis for beginners and advanced players for 2, 3, and 5 days. Many mountain activities besides, like hiking for beginners and seasoned hikers in lovely areas around the U.S., England and Switzerland. Singles and couples.

INTERNATIONAL CONTACT

❑ US Servas Committee

11 S. John Street
New York, NY 10038

Comments: Group arranges for you to stay free for three days in the home of a family somewhere in the world where you learn about each other and share ideas.

Date: 3 nights

Cost: You pay your own airfare

OUTDOORS

❑ American Youth Hostels

35 South 3rd Street
Philadelphia, PA 19106
(215) 925-6004

Activity Location: *U.S. and abroad*

Comments: A worldwide network of 6,000 hostels in 70 countries, costing about $9/day, form the basis for the wonderful group trips sponsored by this group. Day trips, week(s) long trips to famous places (Stonehenge in England) and not-so famous places (castles in Hungary). Also trips in the U.S. Not just for youth.

Cost: Reasonable

❑ Outward Bound USA

384 Field Point Road
Greenwich, CT 06830
(800) 243-8520

Comments: Wilderness outings taught and experienced — such as desert backpacking and canyon exploration, canoeing, sailing, alpine mountaineering, whitewater rafting. All ages and locations. Encourages personal confidence and group skills.

❏ REI Adventures

P.O. Box 1938
Sumner, WA 98390-0800
(800) 622-2236

Comments: Biking, mountain biking, kayaking, backpacking, climbing, walking trips all over the U.S. and the world beyond. Outdoor skills taught. REI is committed to responsible travel: respecting the environment and local people.

❏ Sierra Club

623 Catharine Street
Philadelphia, PA 19147
(215) 592-4063

Comments: National organization sponsors great outdoor activities including: hiking, bike hikes, boating and programs about natural resources (example: weekend natural history expedition to watch bald eagles). Also has a local singles group.

❏ Orienteering Events

U.S. Orienteering Federation
Box 1444
Forest Park, GA 30051

Activity Location: *State parks around the country*

Comments: Orienteering means you use a compass and a topographic map to find your way along a course while looking for checked points on a map. You navigate through woods, along mountain ranges, and over streams on a great discovery trail!

PERSONAL GROWTH

❑ Omega Institute

260 Lake Drive
Rhinebeck, NY 12572
(914) 266-4301

Comments: A wide range of great workshops in health, professional development, art, social action, or spiritual awareness. Examples: "Music Festival," "Rhythmic Village," "Drums of passion," "Playful Community," "Women's Baseball" and more!
Date: Mostly in summer

SENIORS

❑ Elderhostel

80 Boylston Street
Boston, Mass 02116

Activity Location: *Varied college campuses*

Comments: Elderhostel, for people 60 and over, has an awesome program of thousands of educational adventures in all parts of this country and internationally. Some examples of nearby programs are: learning to play the recorder or taking classes in music appreciation at the Peabody Institute in Baltimore; and taking a hiking and biology program on the Appalachian Trail in New Hampshire. Call for huge catalogs that are fun reading.
Date: One week
Cost: Reasonable

❑ World Adventure Trips

Golden Companions
P.O. Box 754
Pullman, WA 99163

Comments: This group of several hundred people matches up traveling companions for people age 50 and older for all kinds of excursions and travel. Members get a list of potential companions, a newsletter and more. Members organize social get-togethers after their trips.
Cost: Membership fee approximately $50

VACATIONS

SINGLES

❑ Club Med

(800) Club Med

Comments: A one-price vacation with all meals, sports and entertainment included. Half singles, half married, guests. 110 vacation villages attract distinct crowds, e.g., Copper Mountain (Colorado) has skiers, Bahamas has tennis players, etc.

❑ Tennis Camps Limited

444 East 82nd Street, Suite 31d
New York, NY 10028
(800) 223-2442

Comments: Tennis camps for singles in Stowe, Vermont. Top notch instruction. Beginners and advanced groups.

SPORTS

❑ Killington School For Tennis

(802) 422-3101

Comments: For novice to expert, this school in the Green Mountains of Vermont puts you in your class and provides accelerated tennis lessons for two, three or five days. Instruction includes video analysis.

UNIVERSITY VACATIONS

❑ American Museum Of Natural History Discovery Tours

Central Park West At 79th Street
New York, NY 10024
(800) 462-8687

Comments: Pricey but high quality trips including: "Great Apes and Great Lakes in Uganda;" "Maya: Ruins & Forests;" "Cruising Through Provence (France)," and more!

❑ Brown's Continuing College

> *Box 1920*
> *Providence, RI 02906*
> *(401) 863-2474*

Comments: Great study vacation program. Topic for 1994 was "Ethnocentrism" and included a lecture by Arthur Schlesinger Jr. Topics: 1: What is ethnocentricism, 2: Case studies of ethnocentricity in several countries, and 3) in the U.S. What a program!
Date: 4 Days in June
Cost: $600-700 for everything
Contact: Don Slack

❑ Cornell's Adult University

> *626 Thurston Avenue*
> *Ithaca, NY 14850*
> *(607) 255-6260*

Comments: Take a single one-week class, taught in half-day sessions. Stay in student lodgings with good meals, great professors and beautiful surroundings. Terrific selection of topics including: "The Republicans From Lincoln To Clinton," "Gorgeous Gorges In The Finger Lakes," and "The Personal Essay: A Writing Workshop."
Date: Summer

❑ Asimov Seminar

> *Rensselaerville Institute*
> *(609) 629-3732*
> *P.O. Box 54*
> *Rensselaerville, NY 12147*

Comments: Provocative seminars on social organizations and policies of a hypothetical outer-space community, a spin off from Asimov's images. You will role play a planetary colonizer to create the perfect society! Led by Asimov experts.
Date: 3 days in July
Contact: Don Mcgrain

❏ Smithsonian Study Tours & Seminars

1100 Jefferson Drive SW, Room 3045
Washington, DC 20560
(202) 357-2627

Comments: Incredible sophisticated learning vacations that broaden your knowledge of particular subjects. Examples: in NYC, "Living And Design;" "American Popular Music (New Orleans);" "Wolf Tracking In Minnesota And Canada."

VACATIONS

— NOTES —

Especially For Women

ADVOCACY & WOMEN'S STUDIES

BOATING

BOOK GROUP

CAREERS

CLASSES

SUPPORTIVE NETWORKS

VACATIONS

WRITING

Gatherings of Business Women talk at a local business fair exhibit. Photo by Ken Kauffman.

WOMEN ONLY

To have a healthy social life, it is really important to have same sex friends: People of your gender with whom you can hang out, go to the movies, play golf, go for long walks, check out River City Blues on Penn's Landing, or just go for a coffee and a shop at the Manayunk Market. This chapter is to give women some ideas about where to find women who can be new friends — perhaps women to join doing new activities.

My view is that when women get together they spend much more time talking about their relationships than they do being active and involved in play, and men tend to do the opposite. I'm not sure why this is, or even if it is accurate, but my wish is that women would play more — lighthearted, forget the serious things, just goof-off stuff with silliness and laughing or doing some interesting sports and games. Similarly, I'd like to see more women involved together in ongoing group activities like canoeing or oil painting or community service. Whatever you choose, I think it's crucial to have a network of same sex friends in your life, people that you can count on to do whatever you love most with. The activities listed here include some great places to network with other women where a specific enjoyable activity is the focus.

Starting with the purely fun things, you can go sailing with WOMEN ONLY with **WAVES/Womanship** out of Annapolis. It has a wonderful sailing school and sailing excursions for beginners and experienced sailors, where the dynamics between men and women are left out! (The sailors among you know what I mean!) It is a great place to learn. **The Executive Women's Golf League** is an association of women from diverse work environments who network around some wonderful golf in the Philadelphia area. They hold clinics, tournaments, and regular golf outings including dinners and socializing.

Some terrific places to meet other women are right under your nose! You can find many women's aerobic classes and other physical activities at your local **"Y"** where you will meet with the women in your neighborhood doing something "for themselves." It's easy to hook up for a coffee or juice after the class with that gal who lives down the street whom you've never had a chance, or "reason," to chat with before. For more far reaching excitement, there are also vacations for women, like the **Killington Ski School** in Vermont, where women teach and learn in a comfortable atmosphere.

Most hobby groups that I've found have been open to both men and women members. Some, however, tend to draw more of one gender than another. For example, women seem to be more involved in gardening groups such as the **Hardy Plant Society** and crafts (e.g., **Phila. Guild of Handweavers**), and men seem to do more games (like chess and GO) and outdoor sports like fly-fishing. But this is not hard and fast by any means. Lots of women are playing SCRABBLE and volleyball these days, and men are active in creating community gardens. So if you are looking to spend some time with same sex people, check with the group that interests you to see about its composition at that time.

In the arts, there is a singing group composed of WOMEN, the **Anna Crusis** choir, which auditions new members from the public. The **Plastic Club**, a local art group, is also primarily a women's group where you can draw and paint with fellow women artists. If you want cultural socializing with single women, Becky O'Neil (**Weekenders**, listed in SINGLES chapter) offers a group that reads together, goes on trips to plays, concerts and historical places, and has good times on the weekends. Take a look at her newsletter to see the interesting plans they have made!

Did you know there are women's literature groups (**Mt. Airy Book Group**) that only read books by and about women?

WOMEN ONLY

One person was instrumental in starting such a group which then spawned several groups of this kind in different areas in and around the city. Shows you what one person can do! Likewise, there are writing groups for women (**"Caring — Nurturing" Writers' Group**) where the unique quality of women's writing is expressed and enjoyed.

There are a growing number of professional organizations for women in the Philadelphia region, one of which, **NAWBO (National Association of Women Business Owners)** recently held its national conference here. This highly professional group has regular meetings featuring speakers, workshops and local networking sessions of value to new and experienced business owners. Another professional group, **Gatherings of Business Women**, holds monthly breakfast meetings in five major areas in the city where business women meet each other, talk about their services, hear speakers from among the membership, and break great breakfast together at local restaurants. It's a good way to start your morning and it's probably close to your house! If you are interested in classes related to your career goals, you can find them at LaSalle University where programs to help women develop their professional skills are offered (**Fresh Start**).

If you've had trouble finding places to meet new women friends, you aren't alone. A number of organizations that understand this difficulty sponsor workshops and discussions that facilitate women connecting. A few include the **Single Women's Group**, based on the Single Booklover's model, **Women Reach** in Center City, and the **Women's Resource Center** in Wayne. This center offers workshops led by experts in the fields and activities that are of interest to women, single and attached. Some are purely for fun, like attending plays and excursions, while others (the open Wednesday night discussion group) address important women's issues. Also, groups such as

Creative Energy Options whose wide variety of programs span all populations, include special personal growth workshops for women. So look for WOMEN ONLY activities as part of the offerings from many groups.

No MEN ONLY chapter? I tried, I really tried. There are occasional workshops listed in the *Welcomat* "Events" section, but the only group I found exclusively for MEN was an established group held at the **Men's Resource Center** by Dr. Gerald Evans, (215 971-9310). It holds support groups, men's discussion groups, and adventure trips. Are there other groups out there?

ADVOCACY & WOMEN'S STUDIES

❑ National Organization For Women

1218 Chestnut Street, Room 308
Philadelphia, PA 19106
(215) 922-6040

Comments: This activist group defends the basic human rights of women. Monthly meetings feature topics like "African-American Feminists" and sometimes have speakers. Other events include open houses and films.

Date: 1st Monday/month   **Time:** 5:30pm

❑ Women's Alliance For Job Equity (WAJE)

1422 Chestnut Street, Suite 1100
Philadelphia, PA
(215) 561-1873

Comments: A group that works to improve economic and workplace conditions for women. They sponsor group discussions and reading/study groups.

BOATING

❑ Womenship

WAVES
The Boathouse, 410 Severn Avenue
Annapolis, MD 21403
(800) 342-9295

Comments: Learn to sail with a community of women teachers and fellow sailors. Sail around Annapolis and after you've learned, sail in the Caribbean!

Cost: About $350-$450 for weekend sails

WOMEN ONLY

BOOK GROUP

❑ Mt. Airy Book Group
(215) 896-8852

Activity Location: *Private homes in East Mt. Airy*

Comments: This group reads good literature by both men and women interested in multiculturalism.
Contact: Candy Margolin

❑ Women & Literature Book Group
(215) 896-8852

Activity Location: *Penn Wynne Library, Penn Wynne, PA*

Comments: Women's group that discusses literature by women, particularly works of fiction.
Date: Thursdays   **Time:** 10am
Contact: Candy Margolin

CAREERS

❑ Gatherings of Business Women
4101 Kelly Drive
Philadelphia, PA 19129
(215) 844-3018

Comments: Terrific monthly organization of business women meets for breakfast in four parts of the city. Come to network your services and hear a speaker who can help you improve your business. You'll like these women!
Contact: Diane Carlson

❑ National Association Of Women Business Owners
(215) 972-1533

Comments: An active Philadelphia branch of a national organization with monthly meetings, excellent networking opportunities and very interesting local programs on developing your business.
Cost: $60 Membership dues

WOMEN ONLY

Classes • Supportive Networks

CLASSES

❏ Fresh Start

LaSalle University Continuing Education For Women
20th Street and Olney Avenue
Philadelphia, PA 19141
(215) 951-1060

Comments: Fresh Start seminars give women a chance to begin or resume their education, including techniques on how to study, and how to juggle work, family and school.

SUPPORTIVE NETWORKS

❏ Heart Of The Goddess

10 Leopard Road
Berwyn, PA 19312
(215) 695-9494

Comments: This wholistic center and gallery offers workshops in "Women's Drumming," "Shakti Woman," "Woman Wisdom," "Motherpeace Tarot," and other programs for women healing.

❏ Philadelphia Women's Network

(215) 676-1244

Activity Location: *Various locations in Philadelphia*

Comments: Speaker lunches with good opportunities for networking and gathering professional information and personal support.

❏ Single Women's Group

> Box 117
> Gradyville, PA 19039
> (215) 358-5049

Comments: Based on the Single Booklovers model, this is a chance for women to meet other women to do things with. In this national group, connections are made by profiles provided to members.
Cost: $20/Month for newsletter and membership
Contact: Bob and Ruth Leach

❏ Women Reach

> *Jewish Family & Children's Service*
> *1610 Spruce Street*
> *Philadelphia, PA 19103*
> *(215) 545-3290*

Comments: Workshops and classes on women's issues.

❏ Women's Center Of Montgomery County

> *Greenwood Avenue & Meetinghouse Road*
> *Jenkintown, PA 19046*
> *(215) 885-5020*

Comments: This group sponsors workshops and discussion groups on topics like: "Books of Interest to Women," "Mature Women's Issues," "Professional Issues," "Black Women's Network," etc.

❏ Women's Resource Center

> *113 W. Wayne Avenue*
> *Wayne, PA 19087*
> *(215) 687-6391*

Comments: First-rate organization for women providing workshops, support groups, as well as social activities like Wednesday night presentation and discussions, book discussions and trips to the performing arts.

VACATIONS

❑ Women's Ski Clinics

Killington Ski Resort
402 Killington Road
Killington, VT 05751
(802) 422-3333

Comments: Weekend packages and 5-day packages for all levels of women skiers including lessons, lift ticket, meals, special speakers, and groups no larger than 5 women.
Contact: Audrey Helpern

WRITING

"Caring— Nurturing" Women's Writers Group

Philadelphia, PA (Washington Square Area)
(215) 629-1214

Comments: Women writers of poetry, fiction, drama, and essays welcome. Call for information.
Date: Periodic   **Time:** 7:30pm

WOMEN ONLY

— NOTES —

WRITING & POETRY

BROWSING BOOK STORES

CONFERENCES FOR WRITERS

HEAR AN AUTHOR

POETRY

READINGS

WRITERS/READERS GROUPS

WRITING & POETRY

Poet Edward Francis at a publication party at the City Book Shop.

WRITING & POETRY

Forward

WRITING and POETRY tell our stories, all of our stories — about our loves, our mothers and kids, our travels and adventures, our dreams and travesties, and the reaches of our souls. When we write, we connect with others and tell them about ourselves. WRITING is also a golden door to new ideas, ways of doing things, and places to go. WRITING activities appeal to people who like to think. Through them we can expand our knowledge and interests both by listening to others' works or by taking pen in hand ourselves!

You can enter WRITING & POETRY activities through so many doors. You can browse in a bookstore, even sit at a cafe table with your book choices, sipping a cup of cappuccino. You can go to readings and listen and chat with the authors and other listeners. Or you can (gulp) read your writings to interested listeners and ask for criticism (or not). You can attend conferences to learn special writing skills. You can join clubs that meet regularly to read certain types of books (e.g., mysteries), or writers' clubs that meet regularly to critique each others' work. These activities represent a spectrum of risk levels as well. I don't know about you, but I would rather have my thumbs cut off than read my personal poetry to anyone. But I love <u>hearing</u> other peoples' poetry and stories, especially when they read them to me. So we can enter at a very safe and soothing level, or in a high exposure, challenging way that gives us special connection with others who are willing to come forward as well. <u>All</u> these ways are fulfilling and important and wonderful — definitely worth doing, especially now that there are so many terrific places in the area to do it.

So how and where?

Another thing I like about WRITING events is that they are often <u>free or dirt cheap</u>. Where a movie costs $6 and a play costs $15 and up, you can listen to an excellent author <u>read to you</u> for free, or for the cost of a coffee. Also, you can find book-type events in <u>many areas</u> around the city. This fortunate situation is largely because of the emergence of the bookstores in city and suburban areas which recently have been very active in drawing us into the writing experience.

Let's look at some of them:

You can hear an author at **Borders** in Center City, Rosemont, Chestnut Hill and New Jersey almost every night of the week. These authors will be talking about Japanese Games, Women's Sexuality, How to Better Your Chances of Getting a Job, Modern Fiction, and more, illustrating the range of topics people write about today! The topics of the day are well publicized in local papers like the *Welcomat* and *City Paper,* as well as the *Daily News* and *The Inquirer,* so you can plan your participation. Borders started the coffee and books social scene and has continued to host a large number of high quality events that are a lot of fun. In addition, they put out a dynamite newsletter describing new books and upcoming events; pick one up at the shop. The other guys on the block are doing a terrific job offering quality events as well. **Barnes & Noble** sponsor ongoing book clubs in several locations that read special topic books, such as the **Romance Book Club** and the **Mystery Book Club**. The **City Book Shop** offers a very active forum two nights a week for writers to read and listeners to enjoy. On Friday nights they even include music with the readings! Easy places to go for a cup of something and take in famous and local culture. Excellent programs are also found for no cost at the **Philadelphia Free Library**, of course, which sponsors a wide diversity of speakers on a regular basis. You can pick up a newsletter at your local branch while you're choosing your free movie video!

If you are an aspiring writer, you will have company galore and many places to share your work. Besides the above places that invite local writers, there are informal salons such as the

WRITING & POETRY

Astral Writers Group where you can read your writing and be informally critiqued. There are also specialty writers groups, such as groups that write mystery or romance, women's stories, Sherlock Holmes (is the **Baker Street Irregulars** still in Philadelphia?) — even a Star Trek group!

And for POETS?

The largest specialty group is for writers of poetry. The city teems with places to read and listen to poetry such as the **Bothy Club,** the **North Star** and the **City Book Shop**. Special mention for **Poets and Prophets** that sponsors regular meetings throughout the year for poetry events.

The explosion of these types of events is a recent happening in our city: the opening of doors for all of us, not just published writers, to listen, think and talk together about prose and poetry, contemporary issues, and art. The cafe-salon venue for people to meet and connect is for you and me.

Let's go for it and keep it alive!

BROWSING BOOK STORES

❏ The Book Trader & Gallery

501 South Street
Philadelphia, PA
(215) 925-0219

Comments: Used book store that especially lends itself to browsing and chatting. Also has openings for contemporary photo exhibits.

CONFERENCES FOR WRITERS

❏ Rutgers-Camden Writers Conference

Fine Arts Complex, Rutgers University
3rd Street Between Cooper & Ben Franklin Bridge
Camden, NJ
(609) 225-6556

Comments: Fiction writing workshops, readings and more.
Cost: Free

❏ Mid-Atlantic Mystery Book Fair & Convention

Holiday Inn
4th & Arch Street
Philadelphia, PA
(215) 923-0211

Comments: Mystery writers converge annually to meet published authors, attend panels and book signings.

❑ 8th Annual Celebration Of Black Writing Conference

Friends of The Free Library of Philadelphia
Logan Square
Philadelphia, PA
(215) 567-4562

Comments: Weekend with many events honoring black writers including a chance to listen to and meet well known authors.
Date: One Saturday in February

❑ Women's Ink

Moonstone
735-9598

Activity Location: *Robin's Bookstore, 108 S. 13th Street, Philadelphia, PA, (215) 735-9600*

Comments: Meet over 40 authors for conversation, presentations and books. Moonstone offers conferences for different groups of writers.
Date: Annual in May   **Time:** 2pm

HEAR AN AUTHOR

❑ Barnes & Noble

1424 Chestnut Street
Philadelphia, PA
(215) 972-8275

Comments: Like most major bookstores, all branches of Barnes & Noble have author appearances, signings and sometimes discussions to spotlight new books. Watch for them in the Welcomat or *Philadelphia Inquirer's* "Weekend" section. They also sponsor mystery and romance book discussion clubs.

WRITING & POETRY

Hear An Author

❏ Borders Book Shop

1727 Walnut Street
Philadelphia, PA
(215) 568-7400

Comments: Everything happens at Borders! Listen to writers or to readings of current best sellers. Also hear local writers reading their works for the first time. Lots of book readers at these gatherings. Other activities include sampling home brew while you survey the beer-making book, playing Hatchi-Tachi (a game), and more!
Date: Call for schedule of events

❏ Free Library Of Philadelphia, Central Branch

19th Street & Logan Square
Philadelphia, PA
(215) 686-5322

Comments: The library sponsors authors reading from their works. Check your local branch for a newsletter of events. The library not only hosts a variety of photography, exhibits, rare books, and illustrations — but also presents topic/discussions on interesting issues like: "Macrobiotics," "Chinese ceramics," and films.
Cost: Free, of course!

❏ Painted Bride Art Center

230 Vine Street
Philadelphia, PA
(215) 925-9914

Comments: The Bride has readings of exciting new works, especially poetry. They sponsor a well-known annual poetry conference. Call to get on their mailing list.

WRITING & POETRY

POETRY

❏ Arnold's Way

> *Main Street In Manayunk*
> *Philadelphia, PA*
> *(215) 483-2266*

Comments: Informal poetry readings on occasional Saturdays, about once a month.

❏ Bothy Club

> *Mermaid Inn*
> *7673 Germantown Avenue*
> *Philadelphia, PA (Chestnut Hill)*
> *(215) 247-9797*

Comments: Come for poetry and story telling. Sign up at 7:30pm to read between 8pm and 9pm. Main event starts at 9pm.
Date: Mondays   **Time:** 7:30-10pm
Contact: Janet Greenwood

❏ Walt Whitman Center

> *2nd and Cooper Streets*
> *Camden, NJ*
> *(609) 757-7276*

Comments: Regular poetry readings and other writing events including workshops and conferences.

❏ City Book Shop

> *1127 Pine Street*
> *Philadelphia, PA*
> *(215) 592-1992*

Comments: Poetry, stories, folk music — share your work or just listen.
Date: Sundays   **Time:** 2pm
Cost: Free

WRITING & POETRY

Poetry

❏ North Star Poetry Series

North Star Bar
27th & Poplar Streets
Philadelphia, PA
(215) 235-7826

Comments: An intermittent series of poetry readings often followed by thoughtful discussions.
Date: Tuesdays

❏ Northeast Poetry Forum

Northeast Philadelphia Cultural Council
(215) 685-0592

Activity Location: *Northeast Library, Cottman Avenue and Oakland Street, Philadelphia, PA*

Comments: The Forum has scheduled open poetry readings by local poets (like you?) and occasional writing clinics. Also held in other locations like the JCC, Klein Branch, Red Lion Road and Jamison Street.
Date: Some Saturdays & Mondays   **Time:** 2pm & 7:30pm

❏ Word Up: CityWide Poetry Festival

Painted Bride Art Center
230 Vine Street
Philadelphia, PA
(215) 925-9914

Comments: One event sponsored by the Pennsylvania Council on the Arts, many organizations (at least 40) brought contributions to this festival for poet enthusiasts. A good way to find poetry groups with different emphases and in various locations.
Cost: $5

WRITING & POETRY

Poetry • Readings

❑ Fiction Writing Workshop

Gershman YM & YWHA Branch
Broad & Pine Streets
Philadelphia, PA 19147
(215) 545-4400

Comments: This four-session workshop is one example of courses offered by this Poetry Center and listed in the *Welcomat*. The Gershman Y also has poetry readings — ask about it.
Date: Wednesdays in February   **Time**: 7-9pm
Cost: $60 for four sessions

❑ Poets & Prophets

(215) 328-Poet

Comments: This is a major poetry group in Philadelphia. They have poetry readings at various locations and occasional open readings. Watch for them in the *Welcomat*.

READINGS

❑ Borders Reading Group

Borders Book Shop
1727 Walnut Street
Philadelphia, PA 19103
(215) 568-7400

Comments: Borders (again) in Center City has a reading group that focuses on contemporary works. You need to sign up at the information desk for a seat.
Date: Monthly

❏ Bothy Club

Mermaid Inn
7673 Germantown Avenue
Philadelphia, PA (Chestnut Hill)
(215) 664-9488

Comments: Cafe with readings and storytelling included at the Bothy Club with open sign-up at 7:30pm to read between 8pm & 9pm. Main event starts at 9pm Mondays
Time: 7:30pm
Cost: $4

❏ City Book Shop

1127 Pine Street
Philadelphia, PA
(215) 592-1992

Comments: This terrific book shop sponsors open readings of poetry and prose on Wednesdays, with the second Wednesday including musicians and performers. Fridays is a featured reading with an established author.
Date: Fridays and 2nd & 4th Wednesdays **Time:** 7pm
Cost: Free

❏ Pen And Pencil Club

1623 Sansom Street, 2nd Floor
Philadelphia, PA
(215) 328-7638

Comments: Periodic readings by local writers often followed by open readings.
Date: Saturdays **Time:** 7pm

WRITING & POETRY

Readings

❑ The Writer's Voice

Temple University Center City
1616 Walnut Street
Philadelphia, PA
(215) 204-1527

Comments: Open readings for writers of prose, poetry, and essays.
Listeners more than welcome!
Date: Mondays   **Time:** 8pm

❑ Writers Cooperative

Temple University Association For Retired Professionals
1616 Walnut Street
Philadelphia, PA
(215) 204-1505

Comments: One of <u>60 courses</u> given by TARP, this class addresses
prose and poetry on alternate weeks. Students sharpen their writing
skills, have group critiques and produce fine works that are published
at the end of the year. Field trips followed by class analyses as well.
For new <u>and</u> experienced writers.
Contact: Carlena Reyes

❑ Poets & Writers Series

Temple University Creative Writing Program
1616/19 Walnut Street
Philadelphia, PA 19103
(215) 204-1796

Comments: Readings by recognized and emerging authors. Meet and
talk with the guest author after the program. Call to receive fliers of
upcoming readings.
Date: Thursdays
Contact: Creative Writing Department

WRITERS/READERS GROUPS

❑ Mystery Book Club

Barnes & Noble Bookstore
720-730 Lancaster Avenue
Bryn Mawr, PA 19010
(215) 520-0355

Comments: Book club discusses British, American and award-winning mystery authors who read for the group. Participants also read and discuss from a reading list and mystery book journal. Writers and readers welcome!
Date: 2nd Wednesday/month   **Time:** 7:30-8:30pm
Contact: Kathy Sicliano

❑ A Festival For Writers

Association Of Main Line Writers' Clubs
P.O. Box 60391
King Of Prussia, PA 19406

Activity Location: *Rosemont College, Montgomery Avenue & Wendover Road, Rosemont, PA*

Comments: Event featuring workshops with nationally known professionals speaking about: "Getting Started in Writing," "Writing Dialogue," "Researching What's Hot," "Children's Writing," "Self-Publishing," and more.
Date: Annual in April
Cost: $55/day

❑ Philadelphia Writers Organization

(215) 649-8918
(215) 649-8866 (Hotline)

Comments: Group for writers to network. They hold monthly meetings and sponsor a yearly conference.

WRITING & POETRY

❑ Romance Readers Club

Barnes & Noble
1424 Chestnut Street
Philadelphia, PA
(215) 972-8275

Comments: Periodic gatherings of those interested in romance novels to hear an author and talk together about romance books. Romance book club at Barnes & Noble in Bryn Mawr, (520-0355) too.

❑ "Caring — Nurturing" Women's Writers Group

Philadelphia, PA (Washington Square Area)
(215) 629-1214

Comments: Writers of poetry, fiction, drama, and essays welcome. Call for information.
Date: Periodic   **Time**: 7:30pm

❑ Writers Workshop - Delaware Valley

Neumann College, Life Center
Aston, PA
(215) 623-0793

Comments: Writers, you can bring your work to read for discussion and criticism. Monthly meetings through June.
Date: 3rd Wednesday/month   **Time**: 9am to noon

❑ Astral Writers Group

(215) 629-1039
Philadelphia, PA (Society Hill)

Comments: Literary salon tradition for writers of poetry and prose. They offer a nurturing ambiance with critiquing by the group and piano accompaniment on request. Listeners welcome!
Date: Saturdays   **Time**: 7:30pm

WRITING & POETRY

— NOTES —

Appendix: Useful Resources
(I'm having trouble ending this book)

◆ Music and Theater

Eastern Pa Theater Council, puts out *STAGE* magazine every month. (215) 565-2094, 9 E Rose Valley Rd, Wallingford, PA 19086

Folk Dance Council of Delaware Valley will send a listing that tells you where you can folk dance every night. c/o Janet Amato, 7011 Sprague St, Phila PA 19119, (215) 248-3521.

Folk Song Society: Folk Music Hotline: (215) 732-9992

Tri-State Jazz Society. This group sponsors performances of Jazz, Swing and Dixieland as well as dance concerts. Members get a Newsletter of Events. P.O. Box 896, Mt Laurel, NJ 08054.

◆ Outdoors

American Birding Association. This national organization has a monthly magazine and newsletter to put you in touch with local birding events. P.O. Box 6599, Colorado Springs, CO, 80934, (800) 634-7736.

Keystone Trails Association, Good source of information about Pennsylvania Trails. Includes maps and guidebooks for state trails. Box 261, Cogan Station, PA 17728-0251.

◆ Seniors

Corestates Bank puts out a great free booklet about resources available to Seniors

Milestones: First Newspaper for Older Americans, is a terrific little paper that lists events and articles about contemporary issues affecting people over 50. It's free! Put out by Robert Epp, 246 S 22nd Street, Philadelphia, PA 19103, (215) 732-9029.

65 Ways to be Involved in International Development, A Retired American's Guide to Participation in Local, National and International Activities, put out by the American Association for International Aging, 1133 20th Street, NW, Washington DC, 20036.

◆ Vacations

Traveling On Your Own, by Eleanor Berman, gives great examples of activity related trips.

Volunteer Vacations by Bill Mcmillan, Chicago Review Press, lists and describes working vacations.

Woodswoman, a quarterly newspaper, is published by a non-profit feminist tour operator who lists travel and womens' outdoor adventures as a valuable means of consciousness-raising. Write to 2550 Pillsbury Avenue S., Minneapolis, Minn. 55404.

Commission on Voluntary Service & Action puts out a book *Invest Yourself: The Catalogue*. If you can take weeks off to do service, this book lists more than 200 organizations that need volunteer help. Box 117, New York, NY, 10009. (800) 356-9315.

◆ Volunteering

Volunteer Action Council puts out a publication that lists volunteer opportunities in the area. (215) 665-2474.

◆ Interaction Stuff - truly useful books

Conversationally Speaking: Tested New Ways to Increase Your Personal and Social Effectiveness, by Alan Garner, Lowell House, LA, 1991.

Flow, by M. Csikszentmihalyi, Harper, NY, 1991.

How to Stop Looking for Somebody Perfect and Find Someone to Love, by Judith Sills, Ballantine Press, NY, 1984.

INDEX